Grammatical Study of The English Language

By

Adam J. Wildermuth

OF THE GRAMMATICAL STUDY OF THE ENGLISH LANGUAGE.

"Grammatica quid est? ars rectè scribendi rectèque loquendi; poetarum enarrationem continens; omnium Scientiarum fons uberrimus. * * * Nostra ætas parum perita rerum veterum, nimis brevi gyro grammaticum sepsit; at apud antiques olim tantum auctoritatis hic ordo habuit, ut censores essent et judices scriptorum omnium soli grammatici; quos ob id etiam Criticos vocabant."—DESPAUTER. *Præf. ad Synt*, fol. 1.

1. Such is the peculiar power of language, that there is scarcely any subject so trifling, that it may not thereby be plausibly magnified into something great; nor are there many things which cannot be ingeniously disparaged till they shall seem contemptible. Cicero goes further: "Nihil est tam incredibile quod non dicendo fiat probabile;"—"There is nothing so incredible that it may not by the power of language be made probable." The study of grammar has been often overrated, and still oftener injuriously decried. I shall neither join with those who would lessen in the public esteem that general system of doctrines, which from time immemorial has been taught as grammar; nor attempt, either by magnifying its practical results, or by decking it out with my own imaginings, to invest it with any artificial or extraneous importance.

2. I shall not follow the footsteps of *Neef,* who avers that, "Grammar and incongruity are identical things," and who, under pretence of reaching the same end by better means, scornfully rejects as nonsense every thing that others have taught under that name; because I am convinced, that, of all methods of teaching, none goes farther than his, to prove the reproachful assertion true. Nor shall I imitate the declamation of *Cardell*; who, at the commencement of his Essay, recommends the general study of language on earth, from the consideration that, "The faculty of speech is the medium of social bliss for superior intelligences in an eternal world;" [51] and who, when he has exhausted censure in condemning the practical instruction of others, thus lavishes praise, in both his grammars, upon that formless, void, and incomprehensible theory of his own: "This application of words," says he, "in their endless use, by one plain rule, to all things which nouns can name, instead of being the fit subject of blind cavil, *is the most sublime theme presented to the intellect on earth. It is the practical intercourse of the soul at once with its God, and with all parts of his works!*"—*Cardell's Gram.,* 12mo, p. 87; *Gram.,* 18mo, p. 49.

3. Here, indeed, a wide prospect opens before us; but he who traces science, and teaches what is practically useful, must check imagination, and be content with sober truth.

"For apt the mind or fancy is to rove
Uncheck'd, and of her roving is no end."—MILTON.

Restricted within its proper limits, and viewed in its true light, the practical science of grammar has an intrinsic dignity and merit sufficient to throw back upon any man who dares openly assail it, the lasting stigma of folly and self-conceit. It is true, the judgements of men are fallible, and many opinions are liable to be reversed by better knowledge: but what has been long established by the unanimous concurrence of the learned, it can hardly be the part of a wise instructor now to dispute. The literary reformer who, with the last named gentleman, imagines "that the persons to whom the civilized world have looked up to for instruction in language were all wrong alike in the main points," [52] intends no middle course of reformation, and must needs be a man either of great merit, or of little modesty.

4. The English language may now be regarded as the common inheritance of about fifty millions of people; who are at least as highly distinguished for virtue, intelligence, and enterprise, as any other equal portion of the earth's population. All these are more or less interested in the purity, permanency, and right use of that language; inasmuch as it is to be, not only the medium of mental intercourse with others for them and their children, but the vehicle of all they value, in the reversion of ancestral honour, or in the transmission of their own. It is even impertinent, to tell a man of any respectability, that the study of this his native language is an object of great importance and interest: if he does not, from these most obvious considerations, feel it to be so, the suggestion will be less likely to convince him, than to give offence, as conveying an implicit censure.

5. Every person who has any ambition to appear respectable among people of education, whether in conversation, in correspondence, in public speaking, or in print, must be aware of the absolute necessity of a competent knowledge of the language in which he attempts to express his thoughts. Many a ludicrous anecdote is told, of persons venturing to use words of which they did not know the proper application; many a ridiculous blunder has been published to the lasting disgrace of the writer; and so intimately does every man's reputation for sense depend upon his skill in the use of language, that it is scarcely possible to acquire the one without the other. Who can tell how much of his own good or ill success, how much of the favour or disregard with which he himself has been treated, may have

depended upon that skill or deficiency in grammar, of which, as often as he has either spoken or written, he must have afforded a certain and constant evidence.[53]

6. I have before said, that to excel in grammar, is but to know better than others wherein grammatical excellence consists; and, as this excellence, whether in the thing itself, or in him that attains to it, is merely comparative, there seems to be no fixed point of perfection beyond which such learning may not be carried. In speaking or writing to different persons, and on different subjects, it is necessary to vary one's style with great nicety of address; and in nothing does true genius more conspicuously appear, than in the facility with which it adopts the most appropriate expressions, leaving the critic no fault to expose, no word to amend. Such facility of course supposes an intimate knowledge of all words in common use, and also of the principles on which they are to be combined.

7. With a language which we are daily in the practice of hearing, speaking, reading, and writing, we may certainly acquire no inconsiderable acquaintance, without the formal study of its rules. All the true principles of grammar were presumed to be known to the learned, before they were written for the aid of learners; nor have they acquired any independent authority, by being recorded in a book, and denominated grammar. The teaching of them, however, has tended in no small degree to settle and establish the construction of the language, to improve the style of our English writers, and to enable us to ascertain with more clearness the true standard of grammatical purity. He who learns only by rote, may speak the words or phrases which he has thus acquired; and he who has the genius to discern intuitively what is regular and proper, may have further aid from the analogies which he thus discovers; but he who would add to such acquisitions the satisfaction of knowing what is right, must make the principles of language his study.

8. To produce an able and elegant writer, may require something more than a knowledge of grammar rules; yet it is argument enough in favour of those rules, that without a knowledge of them no elegant and able writer is produced. Who that considers the infinite number of phrases which words in their various combinations may form, and the utter impossibility that they should ever be recognized individually for the purposes of instruction and criticism, but must see the absolute necessity of dividing words into classes, and of showing, by general rules of formation and construction, the laws to which custom commonly subjects them, or from which she allows them in particular instances to deviate? Grammar, or the art of writing and speaking, must continue to be learned by some persons; because it is of indispensable use to society. And the only question is, whether children and youth shall acquire it by a regular process of study and method of instruction, or be left to glean it solely from their own occasional observation of the manner in which other people speak and write.

9. The practical solution of this question belongs chiefly to parents and guardians. The opinions of teachers, to whose discretion the decision will sometimes be left, must have a certain degree of influence upon the public mind; and the popular notions of the age, in respect to the relative value of different studies, will doubtless bias many to the adoption or the rejection of this. A consideration of the point seems to be appropriate here, and I cannot forbear to commend the study to the favour of my readers; leaving every one, of course, to choose how much he will be influenced by my advice, example, or arguments. If past experience and the history of education be taken for guides, the study of English grammar will not be neglected; and the method of its inculcation will become an object of particular inquiry and solicitude. The English language ought to be learned at school or in colleges, as other languages usually are; by the study of its grammar, accompanied with regular exercises of parsing, correcting, pointing, and scanning; and by the perusal of some of its most accurate writers,

accompanied with stated exercises in composition and elocution. In books of criticism, our language is already more abundant than any other. Some of the best of these the student should peruse, as soon as he can understand and relish them. Such a course, pursued with regularity and diligence, will be found the most direct way of acquiring an English style at once pure, correct, and elegant.

10. If any intelligent man will represent English grammar otherwise than as one of the most useful branches of study, he may well be suspected of having formed his conceptions of the science, not from what it really is in itself, but from some of those miserable treatises which only caricature the subject, and of which it is rather an advantage to be ignorant. But who is so destitute of good sense as to deny, that a graceful and easy conversation in the private circle, a fluent and agreeable delivery in public speaking, a ready and natural utterance in reading, a pure and elegant style in composition, are accomplishments of a very high order? And yet of all these, the proper study of English grammar is the true foundation. This would never be denied or doubted, if young people did not find, under some other name, better models and more efficient instruction, than what was practised on them for grammar in the school-room. No disciple of an able grammarian can ever speak ill of grammar, unless he belong to that class of knaves who vilify what they despair to reach.

11. By taking proper advantage of the ductility of childhood, intelligent parents and judicious teachers may exercise over the studies, opinions, and habits of youth a strong and salutary control; and it will seldom be found in experience, that those who have been early taught to consider grammatical learning as worthy and manly, will change their opinion in after life. But the study of grammar is not so enticing that it may be disparaged in the hearing of the young, without injury. What would be the natural effect of the following sentence, which I quote from a late well-written religious

homily? "The pedagogue and his dunce may exercise their wits correctly enough, in the way of grammatical analysis, on some splendid argument, or burst of eloquence, or thrilling descant, or poetic rapture, to the strain and soul of which not a fibre in their nature would yield a vibration."—*New-York Observer*, Vol. ix, p. 73.

12. Would not the bright boy who heard this from the lips of his reverend minister, be apt the next day to grow weary of the parsing lesson required by his schoolmaster? And yet what truth is there in the passage? One can no more judge of the fitness of language, without regard to the meaning conveyed by it, than of the fitness of a suit of clothes, without knowing for whom they were intended. The grand clew to the proper application of all syntactical rules, is *the sense*; and as any composition is faulty which does not rightly deliver the author's meaning, so every solution of a word or sentence is necessarily erroneous, in which that meaning is not carefully noticed and literally preserved. To parse rightly and fully, is nothing else than to understand rightly and explain fully; and whatsoever is well expressed, it is a shame either to misunderstand or to misinterpret.

13. This study, when properly conducted and liberally pursued, has an obvious tendency to dignify the whole character. How can he be a man of refined literary taste, who cannot speak and write his native language grammatically? And who will deny that every degree of improvement in literary taste tends to brighten and embellish the whole intellectual nature? The several powers of the mind are not so many distinct and separable agents, which are usually brought into exercise one by one; and even if they were, there might be found, in a judicious prosecution of this study, a healthful employment for them all. The *imagination*, indeed, has nothing to do with the elements of grammar; but in the exercise of composition, young fancy may spread her wings as soon as they are fledged; and for this

exercise the previous course of discipline will have furnished both language and taste, as well as sentiment.

14. The regular grammatical study of our language is a thing of recent origin. Fifty or sixty years ago, such an exercise was scarcely attempted in any of the schools, either in this country or in England.[54] Of this fact we have abundant evidence both from books, and from the testimony of our venerable fathers yet living. How often have these presented this as an apology for their own deficiencies, and endeavoured to excite us to greater diligence, by contrasting our opportunities with theirs! Is there not truth, is there not power, in the appeal? And are we not bound to avail ourselves of the privileges which they have provided, to build upon the foundations which their wisdom has laid, and to carry forward the work of improvement? Institutions can do nothing for us, unless the love of learning preside over and prevail in them. The discipline of our schools can never approach perfection, till those who conduct, and those who frequent them, are strongly actuated by that disposition of mind, which generously aspires to all attainable excellence.

15. To rouse this laudable spirit in the minds of our youth, and to satisfy its demands whenever it appears, ought to be the leading objects with those to whom is committed the important business of instruction. A dull teacher, wasting time in a school-room with a parcel of stupid or indolent boys, knows nothing of the satisfaction either of doing his own duty, or of exciting others to the performance of theirs. He settles down in a regular routine of humdrum exercises, dreading as an inconvenience even such change as proficiency in his pupils must bring on; and is well content to do little good for little money, in a profession which he honours with his services merely to escape starvation. He has, however, one merit: he pleases his patrons, and is perhaps the only man that can; for they must needs be of that class to whom moral restraint is tyranny, disobedience to teachers, as

often right as wrong; and who, dreading the expense, even of a school-book, always judge those things to be cheapest, which cost the least and last the longest. What such a man, or such a neighbourhood, may think of English grammar, I shall not stop to ask.

16. To the following opinion from a writer of great merit, I am inclined to afford room here, because it deserves refutation, and, I am persuaded, is not so well founded as the generality of the doctrines with which it is presented to the public. "Since human knowledge is so much more extensive than the opportunity of individuals for acquiring it, it becomes of the greatest importance so to economize the opportunity as to make it subservient to the acquisition of as large and as valuable a portion as we can. It is not enough to show that a given branch of education is useful: you must show that it is the most useful that can be selected. Remembering this, I think it would be expedient to dispense with the formal study of English grammar,—a proposition which I doubt not many a teacher will hear with wonder and disapprobation. We learn the grammar in order that we may learn English; and we learn English whether we study grammars or not. Especially we *shall* acquire a competent knowledge of our own language, if other departments of our education were improved."

17. "A boy learns more English grammar by joining in an hour's conversation with educated people, than in poring for an hour over Murray or Horne Tooke. If he is accustomed to such society and to the perusal of well-written books, he will learn English grammar, though he never sees a word about syntax; and if he is not accustomed to such society and such reading, the 'grammar books' at a boarding-school will not teach it. Men learn their own language by habit, and not by rules: and this is just what we might expect; for the grammar of a language is itself formed from the prevalent habits of speech and writing. A compiler of grammar first observes these habits, and then makes his rules: but if a person is himself

familiar with the habits, why study the rules? I say nothing of grammar as a general science; because, although the philosophy of language be a valuable branch of human knowledge, it were idle to expect that school-boys should understand it. The objection is, to the system of attempting to teach children formally that which they will learn practically without teaching."— JONATHAN DYMOND: *Essays on Morality*, p. 195.

18. This opinion, proceeding from a man who has written upon human affairs with so much ability and practical good sense, is perhaps entitled to as much respect as any that has ever been urged against the study in question. And so far as the objection bears upon those defective methods of instruction which experience has shown to be inefficient, or of little use, I am in no wise concerned to remove it. The reader of this treatise will find their faults not only admitted, but to a great extent purposely exposed; while an attempt is here made, as well as in my earlier grammars, to introduce a method which it is hoped will better reach the end proposed. But it may easily be perceived that this author's proposition to dispense with the formal study of English grammar is founded upon an untenable assumption. Whatever may be the advantages of those purer habits of speech, which the young naturally acquire from conversation with educated people, it is not true, that, without instruction directed to this end, they will of themselves become so well educated as to speak and write grammatically. Their language may indeed be comparatively accurate and genteel, because it is learned of those who have paid some attention to the study; but, as they cannot always be preserved from hearing vulgar and improper phraseology, or from seeing it in books, they cannot otherwise be guarded from improprieties of diction, than by a knowledge of the rules of grammar. One might easily back this position by the citation of some scores of faulty sentences from the pen of this very able writer himself.

19. I imagine there can be no mistake in the opinion, that in exact proportion as the rules of grammar are unknown or neglected in any country, will corruptions and improprieties of language be there multiplied. The "general science" of grammar, or "the philosophy of language," the author seems to exempt, and in some sort to commend; and at the same time his proposition of exclusion is applied not merely to the school-grammars, but *a fortiori* to this science, under the notion that it is unintelligible to school-boys. But why should any principle of grammar be the less intelligible on account of the extent of its application? Will a boy pretend that he cannot understand a rule of English grammar, because he is told that it holds good in all languages? Ancient etymologies, and other facts in literary history, must be taken by the young upon the credit of him who states them; but the doctrines of general grammar are to the learner the easiest and the most important principles of the science. And I know of nothing in the true philosophy of language, which, by proper definitions and examples, may not be made as intelligible to a boy, as are the principles of most other sciences. The difficulty of instructing youth in any thing that pertains to language, lies not so much in the fact that its philosophy is above their comprehension, as in our own ignorance of certain parts of so vast an inquiry;—in the great multiplicity of verbal signs; the frequent contrariety of practice; the inadequacy of memory; the inveteracy of ill habits; and the little interest that is felt when we speak merely of words.

20. The grammatical study of our language was early and strongly recommended by Locke,[55] and other writers on education, whose character gave additional weight to an opinion which they enforced by the clearest arguments. But either for want of a good grammar, or for lack of teachers skilled in the subject and sensible of its importance, the general neglect so long complained of as a grievous imperfection in our methods of education, has been but recently and partially obviated. "The attainment of a correct and elegant style," says Dr. Blair, "is an object which demands

application and labour. If any imagine they can catch it merely by the ear, or acquire it by the slight perusal of some of our good authors, they will find themselves much disappointed. The many errors, even in point of grammar, the many offences against purity of language, which are committed by writers who are far from being contemptible, demonstrate, that a *careful study* of the language is previously requisite, in all who aim at writing it properly."—*Blair's Rhetoric*, Lect. ix, p. 91.

21. "To think justly, to write well, to speak agreeably, are the three great ends of academic instruction. The Universities will excuse me, if I observe, that both are, in one respect or other, defective in these three capital points of education. While in Cambridge the general application is turned altogether on speculative knowledge, with little regard to polite letters, taste, or style; in Oxford the whole attention is directed towards classical correctness, without any sound foundation laid in severe reasoning and philosophy. In Cambridge and in Oxford, the art of speaking agreeably is so far from being taught, that it is hardly talked or thought of. *These defects* naturally produce dry unaffecting compositions in the one; superficial taste and puerile elegance in the other; ungracious or affected speech in both."—DR. BROWN, 1757: *Estimate*, Vol. ii, p. 44.

22. "A grammatical study of our own language makes no part of the ordinary method of instruction, which we pass through in our childhood; and it is very seldom we apply ourselves to it afterward. Yet the want of it will not be effectually supplied by any other advantages whatsoever. Much practice in the polite world, and a general acquaintance with the best authors, are good helps; but alone [they] will hardly be sufficient: We have writers, who have enjoyed these advantages in their full extent, and yet cannot be recommended as models of an accurate style. Much less then will, what is commonly called learning, serve the purpose; that is, a critical knowledge of ancient languages, and much reading of ancient authors: The

greatest critic and most able grammarian of the last age, when he came to apply his learning and criticism to an English author, was frequently at a loss in matters of ordinary use and common construction in his own vernacular idiom."—DR. LOWTH, 1763: *Pref. to Gram.*, p. vi.

23. "To the pupils of our public schools the acquisition of their own language, whenever it is undertaken, is an easy task. For he who is acquainted with several grammars already, finds no difficulty in adding one more to the number. And this, no doubt, is one of the reasons why English engages so small a proportion of their time and attention. It is not frequently read, and is still less frequently written. Its supposed facility, however, or some other cause, seems to have drawn upon it such a degree of neglect as certainly cannot be praised. The students in those schools are often distinguished by their compositions in the learned languages, before they can speak or write their own with correctness, elegance, or fluency. A classical scholar too often has his English style to form, when he should communicate his acquisitions to the world. In some instances it is never formed with success; and the defects of his expression either deter him from appearing before the public at all, or at least counteract in a great degree the influence of his work, and bring ridicule upon the author. Surely these evils might easily be prevented or diminished."—DR. BARROW: *Essays on Education*, London, 1804; Philad., 1825, p. 87.

24. "It is also said that those who know Latin and Greek generally express themselves with more clearness than those who do not receive a liberal education. It is indeed natural that those who cultivate their mental powers, write with more clearness than the uncultivated individual. The mental cultivation, however, may take place in the mother tongue as well as in Latin or Greek. Yet the spirit of the ancient languages, further is declared to be superior to that of the modern. I allow this to be the case; but I do not find that the English style is improved by learning Greek. It is known that

literal translations are miserably bad, and yet young scholars are taught to translate, word for word, faithful to their dictionaries. Hence those who do not make a peculiar study of their own language, will not improve in it by learning, in this manner, Greek and Latin. Is it not a pity to hear, what I have been told by the managers of one of the first institutions of Ireland, that it was easier to find ten teachers for Latin and Greek, than one for the English language, though they proposed double the salary to the latter? Who can assure us that the Greek orators acquired their superiority by their acquaintance with foreign languages; or, is it not obvious, on the other hand, that they learned ideas and expressed them in their mother tongue?"—DR. SPURZHEIM: *Treatise on Education,* 1832, p. 107.

25. "Dictionaries were compiled, which comprised all the words, together with their several definitions, or the sense each one expresses and conveys to the mind. These words were analyzed and classed according to their essence, attributes, and functions. Grammar was made a rudiment leading to the principles of all thoughts, and teaching by simple examples, the general classification of words and their subdivisions in expressing the various conceptions of the mind. Grammar is then the key to the perfect understanding of languages; without which we are left to wander all our lives in an intricate labyrinth, without being able to trace back again any part of our way."—*Chazotte's Essay on the Teaching of Languages,* p. 45. Again: "Had it not been for his dictionary and his grammar, which taught him the essence of all languages, and the natural subdivision of their component parts, he might have spent a life as long as Methuselah's, in learning words, without being able to attain to a degree of perfection in any of the languages."—*Ib.,* p. 50. "Indeed, it is not easy to say, to what degree, and in how many different ways, both memory and judgement may be improved by an intimate acquaintance with grammar; which is therefore, with good reason, made the first and fundamental part of literary education. The greatest orators, the most elegant scholars, and the most accomplished

men of business, that have appeared in the world, of whom I need only mention Cæsar and Cicero, were not only studious of grammar, but most learned grammarians."—DR. BEATTIE: *Moral Science*, Vol. i, p. 107.

26. Here, as in many other parts of my work, I have chosen to be liberal of quotations; not to show my reading, or to save the labour of composition, but to give the reader the satisfaction of some other authority than my own. In commending the study of English grammar, I do not mean to discountenance that degree of attention which in this country is paid to other languages; but merely to use my feeble influence to carry forward a work of improvement, which, in my opinion, has been wisely begun, but not sufficiently sustained. In consequence of this improvement, the study of grammar, which was once prosecuted chiefly through the medium of the dead languages, and was regarded as the proper business of those only who were to be instructed in Latin and Greek, is now thought to be an appropriate exercise for children in elementary schools. And the sentiment is now generally admitted, that even those who are afterwards to learn other languages, may best acquire a knowledge of the common principles of speech from the grammar of their vernacular tongue. This opinion appears to be confirmed by that experience which is at once the most satisfactory proof of what is feasible, and the only proper test of what is useful.

27. It must, however, be confessed, that an acquaintance with ancient and foreign literature is absolutely necessary for him who would become a thorough philologist or an accomplished scholar; and that the Latin language, the source of several of the modern tongues of Europe, being remarkably regular in its inflections and systematic in its construction, is in itself the most complete exemplar of the structure of speech, and the best foundation for the study of grammar in general. But, as the general

OF THE BEST METHOD OF TEACHING GRAMMAR.

"Quomodo differunt grammaticus et grammatista? Grammaticus est qui diligenter, acutè, scienterque possit aut dicere aut scribere, et poetas enarrare: idem literatus dicitur. Grammatista est qui barbaris literis obstrepit, cui abusus pro usu est; Græcis Latinam dat etymologiam, et totus in nugis est: Latinè dicitur literator."—DESPAUTER. *Synt.*, fol. 1.

1. It is hardly to be supposed that any person can have a very clear conviction of the best method of doing a thing, who shall not at first have acquired a pretty correct and adequate notion of the thing to be done. Arts must be taught by artists; sciences, by learned men; and, if Grammar is the science of words, the art of writing and speaking well, the best speakers and writers will be the best teachers of it, if they choose to direct their attention to so humble an employment. For, without disparagement of the many worthy men whom choice or necessity has made schoolmasters, it may be admitted that the low estimation in which school-keeping is commonly held, does mostly exclude from it the first order of talents, and the highest acquirements of scholarship. It is one strong proof of this, that we have heretofore been content to receive our digests of English grammar, either from men who had had no practical experience in the labours of a school-

room, or from miserable modifiers and abridgers, destitute alike of learning and of industry, of judgement and of skill.

2. But, to have a correct and adequate notion of English grammar, and of the best method of learning or teaching it, is no light attainment. The critical knowledge of this subject lies in no narrow circle of observation; nor are there any precise limits to possible improvement. The simple definition in which the general idea of the art is embraced, "Grammar is the art of writing and speaking correctly," however useful in order to fix the learner's conception, can scarcely give him a better knowledge of the thing itself, than he would have of the art of painting, when he had learned from Dr. Webster, that it is "the art of representing to the eye, by means of figures and colors, any object of sight, and sometimes emotions of the mind." The first would no more enable him to write a sonnet, than the second, to take his master's likeness. The force of this remark extends to all the technical divisions, definitions, rules, and arrangements of grammar; the learner may commit them all to memory, and know but very little about the art.

3. This fact, too frequently illustrated in practice, has been made the basis of the strongest argument ever raised against the study of grammar; and has been particularly urged against the ordinary technical method of teaching it, as if the whole of that laborious process were useless. It has led some men, even of the highest talents, to doubt the expediency of that method, under any circumstances, and either to discountenance the whole matter, or invent other schemes by which they hoped to be more successful. The utter futility of the old accidence has been inferred from it, and urged, even in some well-written books, with all the plausibility of a fair and legitimate deduction. The hardships of children, compelled to learn what they did not understand, have been bewailed in prefaces and reviews; incredible things boasted by literary jugglers, have been believed by men of sense; and the sympathies of nature, with accumulated prejudices, have been excited

against that method of teaching grammar, which after all will be found in experience to be at once the easiest, the shortest, and the best. I mean, essentially, the ancient positive method, which aims directly at the inculcation of principles.

4. It has been already admitted, that definitions and rules committed to memory and not reduced to practice, will never enable any one to speak and write correctly. But it does not follow, that to study grammar by learning its principles, or to teach it technically by formal lessons, is of no real utility. Surely not. For the same admission must be made with respect to the definitions and rules of every practical science in the world; and the technology of grammar is even more essential to a true knowledge of the subject, than that of almost any other art. "To proceed upon principles at first," says Dr. Barrow, "is the most compendious method of attaining every branch of knowledge; and the truths impressed upon the mind in the years of childhood, are ever afterwards the most firmly remembered, and the most readily applied."—*Essays*, p. 84. Reading, as I have said, is a part of grammar; and it is a part which must of course precede what is commonly called in the schools the study of grammar. Any person who can read, can learn from a book such simple facts as are within his comprehension; and we have it on the authority of Dr. Adam, that, "The principles of grammar are the first abstract truths which a young mind can comprehend."—*Pref. to Lat. Gram.*, p. 4.

5. It is manifest, that, with respect to this branch of knowledge, the duties of the teacher will vary considerably, according to the age and attainments of his pupils, or according to each student's ability or inclination to profit by his printed guide. The business lies partly between the master and his scholar, and partly between the boy and his book. Among these it may be partitioned variously, and of course unwisely; for no general rule can precisely determine for all occasions what may be expected from each. The

deficiencies of any one of the three must either be supplied by the extraordinary readiness of an other, or the attainment of the purpose be proportionably imperfect. What one fails to do, must either be done by an other, or left undone. After much observation, it seems to me, that the most proper mode of treating this science in schools, is, to throw the labour of its acquisition almost entirely upon the students; to require from them very accurate rehearsals as the only condition on which they shall be listened to; and to refer them to their books for the information which they need, and in general for the solution of all their doubts. But then the teacher must see that he does not set them to grope their way through a wilderness of absurdities. He must know that they have a book, which not only contains the requisite information, but arranges it so that every item of it may be readily found. That knowledge may reasonably be required at their recitations, which culpable negligence alone could have prevented them from obtaining.

6. Most grammars, and especially those which are designed for the senior class of students, to whom a well-written book is a sufficient instructor, contain a large proportion of matter which is merely to be read by the learner. This is commonly distinguished in type from those more important doctrines which constitute the frame of the edifice. It is expected that the latter will receive a greater degree of attention. The only successful method of teaching grammar, is, to cause the principal definitions and rules to be committed thoroughly to memory, that they may ever afterwards be readily applied. Oral instruction may smoothe the way, and facilitate the labour of the learner; but the notion of communicating a competent knowledge of grammar without imposing this task, is disproved by universal experience. Nor will it avail any thing for the student to rehearse definitions and rules of which he makes no practical application. In etymology and syntax, he should be alternately exercised in learning small portions of his book, and then applying them in parsing, till the whole is rendered familiar. To a good

reader, the achievement will be neither great nor difficult; and the exercise is well calculated to improve the memory and strengthen all the faculties of the mind.

7. The objection drawn from the alleged inefficiency of this method, lies solely against the practice of those teachers who disjoin the principles and the exercises of the art; and who, either through ignorance or negligence, impose only such tasks as leave the pupil to suppose, that the committing to memory of definitions and rules, constitutes the whole business of grammar.[56] Such a method is no less absurd in itself, than contrary to the practice of the best teachers from the very origin of the study. The epistle prefixed to King Henry's Grammar almost three centuries ago, and the very sensible preface to the old British Grammar, an octavo reprinted at Boston in 1784, give evidence enough that a better method of teaching has long been known. Nay, in my opinion, the very best method cannot be essentially different from that which has been longest in use, and is probably most known. But there is everywhere ample room for improvement. Perfection was never attained by the most learned of our ancestors, nor is it found in any of our schemes. English grammar can be better taught than it is now, or ever has been. Better scholarship would naturally produce this improvement, and it is easy to suppose a race of teachers more erudite and more zealous, than either we or they.

8. Where invention and discovery are precluded, there is little room for novelty. I have not laboured to introduce a system of grammar essentially new, but to improve the old and free it from abuses. The mode of instruction here recommended is the result of long and successful experience. There is nothing in it, which any person of common abilities will find it difficult to understand or adopt. It is the plain didactic method of definition and example, rule and praxis; which no man who means to teach grammar well, will ever desert, with the hope of finding an other more

rational or more easy. This book itself will make any one a grammarian, who will take the trouble to observe and practise what it teaches; and even if some instructors should not adopt the readiest means of making their pupils familiar with its contents, they will not fail to instruct by it as effectually as they can by any other. A hope is also indulged, that this work will be particularly useful to many who have passed the ordinary period allotted to education. Whoever is acquainted with the grammar of our language, so as to have some tolerable skill in teaching it, will here find almost every thing that is true in his own instructions, clearly embraced under its proper head, so as to be easy of reference. And perhaps there are few, however learned, who, on a perusal of the volume, would not be furnished with some important rules and facts which had not before occurred to their own observation.

9. The greatest peculiarity of the method is, that it requires the pupil to speak or write a great deal, and the teacher very little. But both should constantly remember that grammar is the art of speaking and writing well; an art which can no more be acquired without practice, than that of dancing or swimming. And each should ever be careful to perform his part handsomely—without drawling, omitting, stopping, hesitating, faltering, miscalling, reiterating, stuttering, hurrying, slurring, mouthing, misquoting, mispronouncing, or any of the thousand faults which render utterance disagreeable and inelegant. It is the learner's diction that is to be improved; and the system will be found well calculated to effect that object; because it demands of him, not only to answer questions on grammar, but also to make a prompt and practical application of what he has just learned. If the class be tolerable readers, and have learned the art of attention, it will not be necessary for the teacher to say much; and in general he ought not to take up the time by so doing. He should, however, carefully superintend their rehearsals; give the word to the next when any one errs; and order the exercise in such a manner that either his own voice, or the example of his

best scholars, may gradually correct the ill habits of the awkward, till all learn to recite with clearness, understanding well what they say, and making it intelligible to others.

10. Without oral instruction and oral exercises, a correct habit of speaking our language can never be acquired; but written rules, and exercises in writing, are perhaps quite as necessary, for the formation of a good style. All these should therefore be combined in our course of English grammar. And, in order to accomplish two objects at once, the written doctrines, or the definitions and rules of grammar, should statedly be made the subject of a critical exercise in utterance; so that the boy who is parsing a word, or correcting a sentence, in the hearing of others, may impressively realize, that he is then and there exhibiting his own skill or deficiency in oral discourse. Perfect forms of parsing and correcting should be given him as models, with the understanding that the text before him is his only guide to their right application. It should be shown, that in parsing any particular word, or part of speech, there are just so many things to be said of it, and no more, and that these are to be said in the best manner: so that whoever tells fewer, omits something requisite; whoever says more, inserts something irrelevant; and whoever proceeds otherwise, either blunders in point of fact, or impairs the beauty of the expression. I rely not upon what are called "*Parsing Tables*" but upon the precise forms of expression which are given in the book for the parsing of the several sorts of words. Because the questions, or abstract directions, which constitute the common parsing tables, are less intelligible to the learner than a practical example; and more time must needs be consumed on them, in order to impress upon his memory the number and the sequence of the facts to be stated.

11. If a pupil happen to be naturally timid, there should certainly be no austerity of manner to embarrass his diffidence; for no one can speak well, who feels afraid. But a far more common impediment to the true use of

speech, is carelessness. He who speaks before a school, in an exercise of this kind, should be made to feel that he is bound by every consideration of respect for himself, or for those who hear him, to proceed with his explanation or rehearsal, in a ready, clear, and intelligible manner. It should be strongly impressed upon him, that the grand object of the whole business, is his own practical improvement; that a habit of speaking clearly and agreeably, is itself one half of the great art of grammar; that to be slow and awkward in parsing, is unpardonable negligence, and a culpable waste of time; that to commit blunders in rehearsing grammar, is to speak badly about the art of speaking well; that his recitations must be limited to such things as he perfectly knows; that he must apply himself to his book, till he can proceed without mistake; finally, that he must watch and imitate the utterance of those who speak well, ever taking that for the best manner, in which there are the fewest things that could be *mimicked*.[57]

12. The exercise of parsing should be commenced immediately after the first lesson of etymology—the lesson in which are contained the definitions of the ten parts of speech; and should be carried on progressively, till it embraces all the doctrines which are applicable to it. If it be performed according to the order prescribed in the following work, it will soon make the student perfectly familiar with all the primary definitions and rules of grammar. It asks no aid from a dictionary, if the performer knows the meaning of the words he is parsing; and very little from the teacher, if the forms in the grammar have received any tolerable share of attention. It requires just enough of thought to keep the mind attentive to what the lips are uttering; while it advances by such easy gradations and constant repetitions as leave the pupil utterly without excuse, if he does not know what to say. Being neither wholly extemporaneous nor wholly rehearsed by rote, it has more dignity than a school-boy's conversation, and more ease than a formal recitation, or declamation; and is therefore an exercise well

calculated to induce a habit of uniting correctness with fluency in ordinary speech—a species of elocution as valuable as any other.[58]

13. Thus would I unite the practice with the theory of grammar; endeavouring to express its principles with all possible perspicuity, purity, and propriety of diction; retaining, as necessary parts of the subject, those technicalities which the pupil must needs learn in order to understand the disquisitions of grammarians in general; adopting every important feature of that system of doctrines which appears to have been longest and most generally taught; rejecting the multitudinous errors and inconsistencies with which unskillful hands have disgraced the science and perplexed the schools; remodelling every ancient definition and rule which it is possible to amend, in respect to style, or grammatical correctness; supplying the numerous and great deficiencies with which the most comprehensive treatises published by earlier writers, are chargeable; adapting the code of instruction to the present state of English literature, without giving countenance to any innovation not sanctioned by reputable use; labouring at once to extend and to facilitate the study, without forgetting the proper limits of the science, or debasing its style by puerilities.

14. These general views, it is hoped, will be found to have been steadily adhered to throughout the following work. The author has not deviated much from the principles adopted in the most approved grammars already in use; nor has he acted the part of a servile copyist. It was not his design to introduce novelties, but to form a practical digest of established rules. He has not laboured to subvert the general system of grammar, received from time immemorial; but to improve upon it, in its present application to our tongue. That which is excellent, may not be perfect; and amendment may be desirable, where subversion would be ruinous. Believing that no theory can better explain the principles of our language, and no contrivance afford greater facilities to the student, the writer has in general adopted those

doctrines which are already best known; and has contented himself with attempting little more than to supply the deficiencies of the system, and to free it from the reproach of being itself ungrammatical. This indeed was task enough; for, to him, all the performances of his predecessors seemed meagre and greatly deficient, compared with what he thought needful to be done. The scope of his labours has been, to define, dispose, and exemplify those doctrines anew; and, with a scrupulous regard to the best usage, to offer, on that authority, some further contributions to the stock of grammatical knowledge.

15. Having devoted many years to studies of this nature, and being conversant with most of the grammatical treatises already published, the author conceived that the objects above referred to, might be better effected than they had been in any work within his knowledge. And he persuades himself, that, however this work may yet fall short of possible completeness, the improvements here offered are neither few nor inconsiderable. He does not mean to conceal in any degree his obligations to others, or to indulge in censure without discrimination. He has no disposition to depreciate the labours, or to detract from the merits, of those who have written ably upon this topic. He has studiously endeavoured to avail himself of all the light they have thrown upon the subject. With a view to further improvements in the science, he has also resorted to the original sources of grammatical knowledge, and has not only critically considered what he has seen or heard of our vernacular tongue, but has sought with some diligence the analogies of speech in the structure of several other languages. If, therefore, the work now furnished be thought worthy of preference, as exhibiting the best method of teaching grammar; he trusts it will be because it deviates least from sound doctrine, while, by fair criticism upon others, it best supplies the means of choosing judiciously.

16. Of all methods of teaching grammar, that which has come nearest to what is recommended above, has doubtless been the most successful; and whatever objections may have been raised against it, it will probably be found on examination to be the most analogous to nature. It is analytic in respect to the doctrines of grammar, synthetic in respect to the practice, and logical in respect to both. It assumes the language as an object which the learner is capable of conceiving to be one whole; begins with the classification of all its words, according to certain grand differences which make the several parts of speech; then proceeds to divide further, according to specific differences and qualities, till all the classes, properties, and relations, of the words in any intelligible sentence, become obvious and determinate: and he to whom these things are known, so that he can see at a glance what is the construction of each word, and whether it is right or not, is a good grammarian. The disposition of the human mind to generalize the objects of thought, and to follow broad analogies in the use of words, discovers itself early, and seems to be an inherent principle of our nature. Hence, in the language of children and illiterate people, many words are regularly inflected even in opposition to the most common usage.

17. It has unfortunately become fashionable to inveigh against the necessary labour of learning by heart the essential principles of grammar, as a useless and intolerable drudgery. And this notion, with the vain hope of effecting the same purpose in an easier way, is giving countenance to modes of teaching well calculated to make superficial scholars. When those principles are properly defined, disposed, and exemplified, the labour of learning them is far less than has been represented; and the habits of application induced by such a method of studying grammar, are of the utmost importance to the learner. Experience shows, that the task may be achieved during the years of childhood; and that, by an early habit of study, the memory is so improved, as to render those exercises easy and familiar, which, at a later period, would be found very difficult and irksome. Upon

this plan, and perhaps upon every other, some words will be learned before the ideas represented by them are fully comprehended, or the things spoken of are fully understood. But this seems necessarily to arise from the order of nature in the development of the mental faculties; and an acquisition cannot be lightly esteemed, which has signally augmented and improved that faculty on which the pupil's future progress in knowledge depends.

18. The memory, indeed, should never be cultivated at the expense of the understanding; as is the case, when the former is tasked with ill-devised lessons by which the latter is misled and bewildered. But truth, whether fully comprehended or not, has no perplexing inconsistencies. And it is manifest that that which does not in some respect surpass the understanding, can never enlighten it—can never awaken the spirit of inquiry or satisfy research. How often have men of observation profited by the remembrance of words which, at the time they heard them, they did not "*perfectly understand!*" We never study any thing of which we imagine our knowledge to be perfect. To learn, and, to understand, are, with respect to any science or art, one and the same thing. With respect to difficult or unintelligible phraseology alone, are they different. He who by study has once stored his memory with the sound and appropriate language of any important doctrine, can never, without some folly or conceit akin to madness, repent of the acquisition. Milton, in his academy, professed to teach things rather than words; and many others have made plausible profession of the same thing since. But it does not appear, that even in the hands of Milton, the attempt was crowned with any remarkable success. See *Dr. Barrow's Essays*, p. 85.

19. The vain pretensions of several modern simplifiers, contrivers of machines, charts, tables, diagrams, vincula, pictures, dialogues, familiar lectures, ocular analyses, tabular compendiums, inductive exercises, productive systems, intellectual methods, and various new theories, for the

purpose of teaching grammar, may serve to deceive the ignorant, to amuse the visionary, and to excite the admiration of the credulous; but none of these things has any favourable relation to that improvement which may justly be boasted as having taken place within the memory of the present generation. The definitions and rules which constitute the doctrines of grammar, may be variously expressed, arranged, illustrated, and applied; and in the expression, arrangement, illustration, and application of them, there may be room for some amendment; but no contrivance can ever relieve the pupil from the necessity of committing them thoroughly to memory. The experience of all antiquity is added to our own, in confirmation of this; and the judicious teacher, though he will not shut his eyes to a real improvement, will be cautious of renouncing the practical lessons of hoary experience, for the futile notions of a vain projector.

20. Some have been beguiled with the idea, that great proficiency in grammar was to be made by means of a certain fanciful method of *induction*. But if the scheme does not communicate to those who are instructed by it, a better knowledge of grammar than the contrivers themselves seem to have possessed, it will be found of little use.[59] By the happy method of Bacon, to lead philosophy into the common walks of life, into the ordinary business and language of men, is to improve the condition of humanity; but, in teaching grammar, to desert the plain didactic method of definition and example, rule and praxis, and pretend to lead children by philosophic induction into a knowledge of words, is to throw down the ladder of learning, that boys may imagine themselves to ascend it, while they are merely stilting over the low level upon which its fragments are cast.

21. The chief argument of these inductive grammarians is founded on the principle, that children cannot be instructed by means of any words which they do not perfectly understand. If this principle were strictly true, children

could never be instructed by words at all. For no child ever fully understands a word the first time he hears or sees it; and it is rather by frequent repetition and use, than by any other process, that the meaning of words is commonly learned. Hence most people make use of many terms which they cannot very accurately explain, just as they do of many *things*, the real nature of which they do not comprehend. The first perception we have of any word, or other thing, when presented to the ear or the eye, gives us some knowledge of it. So, to the signs of thought, as older persons use them, we soon attach some notion of what is meant; and the difference between this knowledge, and that which we call an understanding of the word or thing, is, for the most part, only in degree. Definitions and explanations are doubtless highly useful, but induction is not definition, and an understanding of words may be acquired without either; else no man could ever have made a dictionary. But, granting the principle to be true, it makes nothing for this puerile method of induction; because the regular process by definitions and examples is both shorter and easier, as well as more effectual. In a word, this whole scheme of inductive grammar is nothing else than a series of *leading* questions and *manufactured* answers; the former being generally as unfair as the latter are silly. It is a remarkable tissue of ill-laid premises and of forced illogical sequences.

22. Of a similar character is a certain work, entitled, "English Grammar on the *Productive System*: a method of instruction recently adopted in Germany and Switzerland." It is a work which certainly will be "*productive*" of no good to any body but the author and his publishers. The book is as destitute of taste, as of method; of authority, as of originality. It commences with "the *inductive* process," and after forty pages of such matter as is described above, becomes a "*productive* system," by means of a misnamed "RECAPITULATION;" which jumbles together the etymology and the syntax of the language, through seventy-six pages more. It is then made still more "*productive*" by the appropriation of a like space to a reprint

of Murray's Syntax and Exercises, under the inappropriate title, "GENERAL OBSERVATIONS." To Prosody, including punctuation and the use of capitals, there are allotted six pages, at the end; and to Orthography, four lines, in the middle of the volume! (See p. 41.) It is but just, to regard the *title* of this book, as being at once a libel and a lie; a libel upon the learning and good sense of Woodbridge;[60] and a practical lie, as conveying a false notion of the origin of what the volume contains.

23. What there is in Germany or Switzerland, that bears *any resemblance* to this misnamed system of English Grammar, remains to be shown. It would be prodigal of the reader's time, and inconsistent with the studied brevity of this work, to expose the fallacy of what is pretended in regard to the origin of this new method. Suffice it to say, that the anonymous and questionable account of the "Productive System of Instruction," which the author has borrowed from a "valuable periodical," to save himself the trouble of writing a preface, and, as he says, to "*assist* [the reader] in forming an opinion of the comparative merits of *the system*" is not only destitute of all authority, but is totally irrelevant, except to the whimsical *name* of his book. If every word of it be true, it is insufficient to give us even the slightest reason to suppose, that any thing analogous to his production ever had existence in either of those countries; and yet it is set forth on purpose to convey the idea that such a system "*now predominates*" in the schools of both. (See *Pref.*, p. 5.) The infidel *Neef*, whose new method of education has been tried in our country, and with its promulgator forgot, was an accredited disciple of this boasted "productive school;" a zealous coadjutor with Pestalozzi himself, from whose halls he emanated to "teach the offspring of a free people"—to teach them the nature of things sensible, and a contempt for all the wisdom of *books*. And what similarity is there between his method of teaching and that of *Roswell C. Smith*, except their pretence to a common parentage, and that both are worthless?

24. The success of Smith's Inductive and Productive Grammars, and the fame perhaps of a certain "Grammar in Familiar Lectures," produced in 1836 a rival work from the hands of a gentleman in New Hampshire, entitled, "An Analytical Grammar of the English Language, embracing the *Inductive and Productive Methods of Teaching,* with *Familiar Explanations in the Lecture Style*" &c. This is a fair-looking duodecimo volume of three hundred pages, the character and pretensions of which, if they could be clearly stated, would throw further light upon the two fallacious schemes of teaching mentioned above. For the writer says, "This grammar professes *to combine* both the *Inductive* and *Productive* methods of imparting instruction, of which much has been said within a few years *past*"—*Preface,* p. iv. And again: "The inductive and productive methods of instruction contain the essence of modern improvements."—*Gram.,* p. 139. In what these modern improvements consist, he does not inform us; but, it will be seen, that he himself claims the *copyright* of *all* the improvements which he allows to *English grammar* since the appearance of Murray in 1795. More than two hundred pretenders to such improvements, appear however within the time; nor is the grammarian of Holdgate the least positive of the claimants. This new purveyor for the public taste, dislikes the catering of his predecessor, who poached in the fields of Murray; and, with a tacit censure upon *his productions,* has *honestly bought* the rareties which he has served up. In this he has the advantage. He is a better writer too than some who make grammars; though no adept at composition, and a total stranger to method. To call his work a "*system*" is a palpable misnomer; to tell what it is, an impossibility. It is a grammatical chaos, bearing such a resemblance to Smith's or Kirkham's as one mass of confusion naturally bears to an other, yet differing from both in almost every thing that looks like order in any of the three.

25. The claimant of the combination says, "this new system of English grammar now offered to the public, embraces *the principles* of a

'Systematic Introduction to English Grammar,' by John L. Parkhurst; and the *present author* is indebted to Mr. Parkhurst for a knowledge of *the manner* of applying the principles involved in *his peculiar method* of teaching grammatical science. He is also under obligations to Mr. Parkhurst for many useful hints received several years since while under his instruction.—The *copy right* of Parkhurst's Grammar has been purchased by the writer of this, who alone is responsible for the present application of *its definitions.* Parkhurst's Systematic Introduction to English Grammar has passed through two editions, and is *the first improved system* of English grammar that has appeared before the public *since the first introduction* of Lindley Murray's English Grammar."—*Sanborn's Gram., Preface*, p. iii. What, then, is "THE PRODUCTIVE SYSTEM?" and with whom did it originate? The thousands of gross blunders committed by its professors, prove at least that it is no system of writing grammatically; and, whether it originated with Parkhurst or with Pestalozzi, with Sanborn or with Smith, as it is confessedly a method but "recently adopted," and, so far as appears, never fairly tested, so is it a method that needs only to be *known*, to be immediately and forever exploded.

26. The best instruction is that which ultimately gives the greatest facility and skill in practice; and grammar is best taught by that process which brings its doctrines most directly home to the habits as well as to the thoughts of the pupil—which the most effectually conquers inattention, and leaves the deepest impress of shame upon blundering ignorance. In the language of some men, there is a vividness, an energy, a power of expression, which penetrates even the soul of dullness, and leaves an impression both of words unknown and of sentiments unfelt before. Such men can teach; but he who kindly or indolently accommodates himself to ignorance, shall never be greatly instrumental in removing it. "The colloquial barbarisms of boys," says Dr. Barrow, "should never be suffered to pass without notice and censure. Provincial tones and accents, and all

defects in articulation, should be corrected whenever they are heard; lest they grow into established habits, unknown, from their familiarity, to him who is guilty of them, and adopted by others, from the imitation of his manner, or their respect for his authority."—*Barrow's Essays on Education*, p. 88.

27. In the whole range of school exercises, there is none of greater importance than that of parsing; and yet perhaps there is none which is, in general, more defectively conducted. Scarcely less useful, as a means of instruction, is the practice of correcting false syntax orally, by regular and logical forms of argument; nor does this appear to have been more ably directed towards the purposes of discipline. There is so much to be done, in order to effect what is desirable in the management of these things; and so little prospect that education will ever be generally raised to a just appreciation of that study which, more than all others, forms the mind to habits of correct thinking; that, in reflecting upon the state of the science at the present time, and upon the means of its improvement, the author cannot but sympathize, in some degree, with the sadness of the learned Sanctius; who tells us, that he had "always lamented, and often with tears, that while other branches of learning were excellently taught, grammar, which is the foundation of all others, lay so much neglected, and that for this neglect there seemed to be no adequate remedy."—*Pref. to Minerva*. The grammatical use of language is in sweet alliance with the moral; and a similar regret seems to have prompted the following exclamation of the Christian poet:

"Sacred Interpreter of human thought,
How few respect or use thee as they ought!"—COWPER.

28. No directions, either oral or written, can ever enable the heedless and the unthinking to speak or write well. That must indeed be an admirable

book, which can attract levity to sober reflection, teach thoughtlessness the true meaning of words, raise vulgarity from its fondness for low examples, awaken the spirit which attains to excellency of speech, and cause grammatical exercises to be skillfully managed, where teachers themselves are so often lamentably deficient in them. Yet something may be effected by means of better books, if better can be introduced. And what withstands?— Whatever there is of ignorance or error in relation to the premises. And is it arrogant to say there is much? Alas! in regard to this, as well as to many a weightier matter, one may too truly affirm, *Multa non sunt sicut multis videntur*—Many things are not as they seem to many. Common errors are apt to conceal themselves from the common mind; and the appeal to reason and just authority is often frustrated, because a wrong head defies both. But, apart from this, there are difficulties: multiplicity perplexes choice; inconvenience attends change; improvement requires effort; conflicting theories demand examination; the principles of the science are unprofitably disputed; the end is often divorced from the means; and much that belies the title, has been published under the name.

29. It is certain, that the printed formularies most commonly furnished for the important exercises of parsing and correcting, are either so awkwardly written or so negligently followed, as to make grammar, in the mouths of our juvenile orators, little else than a crude and faltering jargon. Murray evidently intended that his book of exercises should be constantly used with his grammar; but he made the examples in the former so dull and prolix, that few learners, if any, have ever gone through the series agreeably to his direction. The publishing of them in a separate volume, has probably given rise to the absurd practice of endeavouring to teach his grammar without them. The forms of parsing and correcting which this author furnishes, are also misplaced; and when found by the learner, are of little use. They are so verbose, awkward, irregular, and deficient, that the pupil must be either a dull boy or utterly ignorant of grammar, if he cannot

express the facts extemporaneously in better English. They are also very meagre as a whole, and altogether inadequate to their purpose; many things that frequently occur in the language, not being at all exemplified in them, or even explained in the grammar itself. When we consider how exceedingly important it is, that the business of a school should proceed without loss of time, and that, in the oral exercises here spoken of, each pupil should go through his part promptly, clearly, correctly, and fully, we cannot think it a light objection that these forms, so often to be repeated, are so badly written. Nor does the objection lie against this writer only: "*Ab uno disce omnes.*" But the reader may demand some illustrations.[61]

30. First—from his etymological parsing: "O Virtue! how amiable thou art!" Here his form for the word *Virtue* is—"*Virtue* is a *common substantive, of* the *neuter* gender, *of the third* person, *in the* singular number, *and the* nominative case."—*Murray's Gram.*, 8vo, Vol. ii, p. 2. It should have been —"*Virtue* is a common *noun*, personified *proper,* of the *second* person, singular number, *feminine* gender, and nominative case." And then the definitions of all these things should have followed in regular numerical order. He gives the class of this noun wrong, for virtue addressed becomes an individual; he gives the gender wrong, and in direct contradiction to what he says of the word in his section on gender; he gives the person wrong, as may be seen by the pronoun *thou*, which represents it; he repeats the definite article three times unnecessarily, and inserts two needless prepositions, making them different where the relation is precisely the same: and all this, in a sentence of two lines, to tell the properties of the noun *Virtue!*—But further: in etymological parsing, the definitions explaining the properties of the parts of speech, ought to be regularly and rapidly rehearsed by the pupil, till all of them become perfectly familiar; and till he can discern, with the quickness of thought, what alone will be true for the full description of any word in any intelligible sentence. All

these the author omits; and, on account of this omission, his whole method of etymological parsing is, miserably deficient.[62]

31. Secondly—from his syntactical parsing: "*Vice* degrades us." Here his form for the word *Vice* is—"*Vice* is a common substantive, *of* the third person, *in the* singular number, *and the* nominative case."—*Murray's Gram.*, 8vo, Vol. ii, p. 9. Now, when the learner is told that this is the syntactical parsing of a noun, and the other the etymological, he will of course conclude, that to advance from the etymology to the syntax of this part of speech, is merely, *to omit the gender*—this being the only difference between the two forms. But even this difference had no other origin than the compiler's carelessness in preparing his octavo book of exercises—the gender being inserted in the duodecimo. And what then? Is the syntactical parsing of a noun to be precisely the same as the etymological? Never. But Murray, and all who admire and follow his work, are content to parse many words by halves—making, or pretending to make, a necessary distinction, and yet often omitting, in both parts of the exercise, every thing which constitutes the difference. He should here have said—"*Vice* is a common noun, of the third person, singular number, neuter gender, and nominative case: and is the subject of *degrades*; according to the rule which says, 'A noun or a pronoun which is the subject of a verb, must be in the nominative case.' Because the meaning is—*vice degrades*." This is the whole description of the word, with its construction; and to say less, is to leave the matter unfinished.

32. Thirdly—from his "Mode of verbally correcting erroneous sentences:" Take his first example: "The man is prudent which speaks little." (How far silence is prudence, depends upon circumstances: I waive that question.) The learner is here taught to say, "This sentence is incorrect; because *which* is a pronoun *of the neuter gender, and does not agree in gender* with its antecedent *man,* which is masculine. But a pronoun should

agree with its antecedent in gender, &c. according to the fifth rule of syntax. *Which* should *therefore* be *who*, a relative pronoun, agreeing with its antecedent *man*; and the sentence should stand thus: 'The man is prudent *who* speaks little.'"—*Murray's Octavo Gram.*, Vol. ii, p. 18; *Exercises*, 12mo, p. xii. Again: "'After I visited Europe, I returned to America.' This sentence," says Murray, "*is not correct*; because the verb *visited* is in the imperfect tense, and yet used here to express an action, not only past, but prior to the time referred to by the verb *returned*, to which it relates. By the thirteenth rule of syntax, when verbs are used that, in point of time, relate to each other, the order of time should be observed. The imperfect tense *visited* should therefore have been *had visited*, in the pluperfect tense, representing the action of *visiting*, not only as past, but also as prior to the time of *returning. The sentence corrected would stand thus*: 'After I *had visited* Europe, I returned to America.'"—*Gr.*, ii, p. 19; *and Ex.* 12mo, p. xii. These are the first two examples of Murray's verbal corrections, and the only ones retained by Alger, in his *improved, recopy-righted edition* of Murray's Exercises. Yet, in each of them, is the argumentation palpably false! In the former, truly, *which* should be *who*; but not because *which* is "of the *neuter gender*;" but because the application of that relative to *persons*, is now nearly obsolete. Can any grammarian forget that, in speaking of brute animals, male or female, we commonly use *which*, and never *who*? But if *which* must needs be *neuter*, the world is wrong in this.— As for the latter example, it is right as it stands; and the correction is, in some sort, tautological. The conjunctive adverb *after* makes one of the actions subsequent to the other, and gives to the *visiting* all the priority that is signified by the pluperfect tense. "*After* I *visited* Europe," is equivalent to "*When* I *had visited* Europe." The whole argument is therefore void.[63]

33. These few brief illustrations, out of thousands that might be adduced in proof of the faultiness of the common manuals, the author has reluctantly introduced, to show that even in the most popular books, with all the

pretended improvements of revisers, the grammar of our language has never been treated with that care and ability which its importance demands. It is hardly to be supposed that men unused to a teacher's duties, can be qualified to compose such books as will most facilitate his labours. Practice is a better pilot than theory. And while, in respect to grammar, the consciousness of failure is constantly inducing changes from one system to another, and almost daily giving birth to new expedients as constantly to end in the same disappointment; perhaps the practical instructions of an experienced teacher, long and assiduously devoted to the study, may approve themselves to many, as seasonably supplying the aid and guidance which they require.

34. From the doctrines of grammar, novelty is rigidly excluded. They consist of details to which taste can lend no charm, and genius no embellishment. A writer may express them with neatness and perspicuity—their importance alone can commend them to notice. Yet, in drawing his illustrations from the stores of literature, the grammarian may select some gems of thought, which will fasten on the memory a worthy sentiment, or relieve the dullness of minute instruction. Such examples have been taken from various authors, and interspersed through the following pages. The moral effect of early lessons being a point of the utmost importance, it is especially incumbent on all those who are endeavouring to confer the benefits of intellectual culture, to guard against the admission or the inculcation of any principle which may have an improper tendency, and be ultimately prejudicial to those whom they instruct. In preparing this treatise for publication, the author has been solicitous to avoid every thing that could be offensive to the most delicate and scrupulous reader; and of the several thousands of quotations introduced for the illustration or application of the principles of the science, he trusts that the greater part will be considered valuable on account of the sentiments they contain.

35. The nature of the subject almost entirely precludes invention. The author has, however, aimed at that kind and degree of originality which are to be commended in works of this sort. What these are, according to his view, he has sufficiently explained in a preceding chapter. And, though he has taken the liberty of a grammarian, to think for himself and write in a style of his own, he trusts it will be evident that few have excelled him in diligence of research, or have followed more implicitly the dictates of that authority which gives law to language. In criticising the critics and grammatists of the schools, he has taken them upon their own ground— showing their errors, for the most part, in contrast with the common principles which they themselves have taught; and has hoped to escape censure, in his turn, not by sheltering himself under the name of a popular master, but by a diligence which should secure to his writings at least the humble merit of self-consistency. His progress in composing this work has been slow, and not unattended with labour and difficulty. Amidst the contrarieties of opinion, that appear in the various treatises already before the public, and the perplexities inseparable from so complicated a subject, he has, after deliberate consideration, adopted those views and explanations which appeared to him the least liable to objection, and the most compatible with his ultimate object—the production of a work which should show, both extensively and accurately, what is, and what is not, good English.

36. The great art of meritorious authorship lies chiefly in the condensation of much valuable thought into few words. Although the author has here allowed himself ampler room than before, he has still been no less careful to store it with such information as he trusted would prevent the ingenious reader from wishing its compass less. He has compressed into this volume the most essential parts of a mass of materials in comparison with which the book is still exceedingly small. The effort to do this, has greatly multiplied his own labour and long delayed the promised publication; but in proportion as this object has been reached, the time and

patience of the student must have been saved. Adequate compensation for this long toil, has never been expected. Whether from this performance any profit shall accrue to the author or not, is a matter of little consequence; he has neither written for bread, nor on the credit of its proceeds built castles in the air. His ambition was, to make an acceptable book, by which the higher class of students might be thoroughly instructed, and in which the eyes of the critical would find little to condemn. He is too well versed in the history of his theme, too well aware of the precarious fortune of authors, to indulge in any confident anticipations of extraordinary success: yet he will not deny that his hopes are large, being conscious of having cherished them with a liberality of feeling which cannot fear disappointment. In this temper he would invite the reader to a thorough perusal of these pages.

37. A grammar should speak for itself. In a work of this nature, every word or tittle which does not recommend the performance to the understanding and taste of the skillful, is, so far as it goes, a certificate against it. Yet if some small errors shall have escaped detection, let it be recollected that it is almost impossible to compose and print, with perfect accuracy, a work of this size, in which so many little things should be observed, remembered, and made exactly to correspond. There is no human vigilance which multiplicity may not sometimes baffle, and minuteness sometimes elude. To most persons grammar seems a dry and difficult subject; but there is a disposition of mind, to which what is arduous, is for that very reason alluring. "Quo difficilius, hoc præclarius," says Cicero; "The more difficult, the more honourable." The merit of casting up a highway in a rugged land, is proportionate not merely to the utility of the achievement, but to the magnitude of the obstacles to be overcome. The difficulties encountered in boyhood from the use of a miserable epitome and the deep impression of a few mortifying blunders made in public, first gave the author a fondness for grammar; circumstances having since favoured this turn of his genius, he has voluntarily pursued the study, with

an assiduity which no man will ever imitate for the sake of pecuniary recompense.

OF GRAMMATICAL DEFINITIONS.

"Scientiam autem nusquam esse censebant, nisi in animi motionibus atque rationibus: quâ de causâ *definitiones* rerum probabant, et has ad omnia, de quibus disceptabatur, adhibebant."—CICERONIS *Academica*, Lib. i, 9.

1. "The first and highest philosophy," says Puffendorf, "is that which delivers the most accurate and comprehensive *definitions* of things." Had all the writers on English grammar been adepts in this philosophy, there would have been much less complaint of the difficulty and uncertainty of the study. "It is easy," says Murray, "to advance plausible objections against almost every definition, rule, and arrangement of grammar."—*Gram.*, 8vo, p. 59. But, if this is true, as regards his, or any other work, the reason, I am persuaded, is far less inherent in the nature of the subject than many have supposed.[64] Objectionable definitions and rules are but evidences of the ignorance and incapacity of him who frames them. And if the science of grammar has been so unskillfully treated that almost all its positions may be plausibly impugned, it is time for some attempt at a reformation of the code. The language is before us, and he who knows most about it, can best prescribe the rules which we ought to observe in the use of it. But how can we expect children to deduce from a few particulars an accurate notion of

general principles and their exceptions, where learned doctors have so often faltered? Let the abettors of grammatical "*induction*" answer.

2. Nor let it be supposed a light matter to prescribe with certainty the principles of grammar. For, what is requisite to the performance? To know certainly, in the first place, what is the *best usage.* Nor is this all. Sense and memory must be keen, and tempered to retain their edge and hold, in spite of any difficulties which the subject may present. To understand things exactly as they are; to discern the differences by which they may be distinguished, and the resemblances by which they ought to be classified; to know, through the proper evidences of truth, that our ideas, or conceptions, are rightly conformable to the nature, properties, and relations, of the objects of which we think; to see how that which is complex may be resolved into its elements, and that which is simple may enter into combination; to observe how that which is consequent may be traced to its cause, and that which is regular be taught by rule; to learn from the custom of speech the proper connexion between words and ideas, so as to give to the former a just application, to the latter an adequate expression, and to things a just description; to have that penetration which discerns what terms, ideas, or things, are definable, and therefore capable of being taught, and what must be left to the teaching of nature: these are the essential qualifications for him who would form good definitions; these are the elements of that accuracy and comprehensiveness of thought, to which allusion has been made, and which are characteristic of "the first and highest philosophy."

3. Again, with reference to the cultivation of the mind, I would add: To observe accurately the appearances of things, and the significations of words; to learn first principles first, and proceed onward in such a manner that every new truth may help to enlighten and strengthen the understanding; and thus to comprehend gradually, according to our

capacity, whatsoever may be brought within the scope of human intellect:—to do these things, I say, is, to ascend by sure steps, so far as we may, from the simplest elements of science—which, in fact, are our own, original, undefinable notices of things—towards the very topmost height of human wisdom and knowledge. The ancient saying, that truth lies hid, or in the bottom of a well, must not be taken without qualification; for "the first and highest philosophy" has many principles which even a child may understand. These several suggestions, the first of which the Baron de Puffendorf thought not unworthy to introduce his great work on the Law of Nature and of Nations, the reader, if he please, may bear in mind, as he peruses the following digest of the laws and usages of speech.

4. "Definitions," says Duncan, in his Elements of Logic, "are intended to make known the meaning of words standing for *complex ideas*;[65] and were we always careful to form those ideas exactly in our minds, and copy our definitions from that appearance, much of the confusion and obscurity complained of in languages might be prevented."—P. 70. Again he says: "The writings of the mathematicians are a clear proof, how much the advancement of human knowledge depends upon a right use of definitions."—P. 72. Mathematical science has been supposed to be, in its own nature, that which is best calculated to develop and strengthen the reasoning faculty; but, as speech is emphatically *the discourse of reason*, I am persuaded, that had the grammarians been equally clear and logical in their instructions, their science would never have been accounted inferior in this respect. Grammar is perhaps the most comprehensive of all studies; but it is chiefly owing to the unskillfulness of instructors, and to the errors and defects of the systems in use, that it is commonly regarded as the most dry and difficult.

5. "Poor Scaliger (who well knew what a definition should be) from his own melancholy experience exclaimed—'*Nihil infelicius grammatico*

definitore!' Nothing is more unhappy than the grammatical definer."—
Tooke's Diversions, Vol. i, p. 238. Nor do our later teachers appear to have
been more fortunate in this matter. A majority of all the definitions and
rules contained in the great multitude of English grammars which I have
examined, are, in some respect or other, erroneous. The nature of their
multitudinous faults, I must in general leave to the discernment of the
reader, except the passages be such as may be suitably selected for
examples of false syntax. Enough, however, will be exhibited, in the course
of this volume, to make the foregoing allegation credible; and of the rest a
more accurate judgement may perhaps be formed, when they shall have
been compared with what this work will present as substitutes. The
importance of giving correct definitions to philological terms, and of stating
with perfect accuracy whatsoever is to be learned as doctrine, has never
been duly appreciated. The grand source of the disheartening difficulties
encountered by boys in the study of grammar, lies in their ignorance of the
meaning of words. This cause of embarrassment is not to be shunned and
left untouched; but, as far as possible, it ought to be removed. In teaching
grammar, or indeed any other science, we cannot avoid the use of many
terms to which young learners may have attached no ideas. Being little
inclined or accustomed to reflection, they often hear, read, or even rehearse
from memory, the plainest language that can be uttered, and yet have no
very distinct apprehension of what it means. What marvel then, that in a
study abounding with terms taken in a peculiar or technical sense, many of
which, in the common manuals, are either left undefined, or are explained
but loosely or erroneously, they should often be greatly puzzled, and
sometimes totally discouraged?

6. *Simple ideas* are derived, not from teaching, but from sensation or
consciousness; but *complex ideas*, or the notions which we have of such
things as consist of various parts, or such as stand in any known relations,
are definable. A person can have no better definition of *heat*, or of *motion*,

than what he will naturally get by *moving* towards a *fire*. Not so of our complex or general ideas, which constitute science. The proper objects of scientific instruction consist in those genuine perceptions of pure mind, which form the true meaning of generic names, or common nouns; and he who is properly qualified to teach, can for the most part readily tell what should be understood by such words. But are not many teachers too careless here? For instance: a boy commencing the process of calculation, is first told, that, "Arithmetic is the art of computing by numbers," which sentence he partly understands; but should he ask his teacher, "What is a *number*, in arithmetic?" what answer will he get? Were Goold Brown so asked, he would simply say, "*A number, in arithmetic, is an expression that tells how many*;" for every expression that tells how many, is a number in arithmetic, and nothing else is. But as no such definition is contained in *the books*,[66] there are ten chances to one, that, simple as the matter is, the readiest master you shall find, will give an erroneous answer. Suppose the teacher should say, "That is a question which I have not thought of; turn to your dictionary." The boy reads from Dr. Webster: "NUMBER—the designation of a unit in reference to other units, or in reckoning, counting, enumerating."—"Yes," replies the master, "that is it; Dr. Webster is unrivalled in giving definitions." Now, has the boy been instructed, or only puzzled? Can he conceive how the number *five* can be a *unit*? or how the word *five*, the figure 5, or the numeral letter V, is "the designation of a *unit*?" He knows that each of these is a number, and that the oral monosyllable *five* is the same number, in an other form; but is still as much at a loss for a proper answer to his question, as if he had never seen either schoolmaster or dictionary. So is it with a vast number of the simplest things in grammar.

7. Since what we denominate scientific terms, are seldom, if ever, such as stand for ideas simple and undefinable; and since many of those which represent general ideas, or classes of objects, may be made to stand for

more or fewer things, according to the author's notion of classification; it is sufficiently manifest that the only process by which instruction can effectually reach the understanding of the pupil and remove the difficulties spoken of, is that of delivering accurate definitions. These are requisite for the information and direction of the learner; and these must be thoroughly impressed upon his mind, as the only means by which he can know exactly how much and what he is to understand by our words. The power which we possess, of making known all our complex or general ideas of things by means of definitions, is a faculty wisely contrived in the nature of language, for the increase and spread of science; and, in the hands of the skillful, it is of vast avail to these ends. It is "the first and highest philosophy," instructing mankind, to think clearly and speak accurately; as well as to know definitely, in the unity and permanence of a general nature, those things which never could be known or spoken of as the individuals of an infinite and fleeting multitude.

8. And, without contradiction, the shortest and most successful way of teaching the young mind to distinguish things according to their proper differences, and to name or describe them aright, is, to tell in direct terms what they severally are. Cicero intimates that all instruction appealing to reason ought to proceed in this manner: "Omnis enim quse à ratione suscipitur de re aliqua institutio, debet à *definitione* proficisci, ut intelligatur quid sit id, de quo disputetur."—*Off*. Lib. i, p. 4. Literally thus: "For all instruction which from reason is undertaken concerning any thing, ought to proceed from a *definition*, that it may be understood what the thing is, about which the speaker is arguing." Little advantage, however, will be derived from any definition, which is not, as Quintilian would have it, "Lucida et succincta rei descriptio,"—"a clear and brief description of the thing."

9. Let it here be observed that scientific definitions are of *things*, and not merely of *words*; or if equally of words *and* things, they are rather of nouns

than of the other parts of speech. For a definition, in the proper sense of the term, consists not in a mere change or explanation of the verbal sign, but in a direct and true answer to the question, What is such or such a thing? In respect to its extent, it must with equal exactness include every thing which comes under the name, and exclude every thing which does not come under the name: then will it perfectly serve the purpose for which it is intended. To furnish such definitions, (as I have suggested,) is work for those who are capable of great accuracy both of thought and expression. Those who would qualify themselves for teaching any particular branch of knowledge, should make it their first concern to acquire clear and accurate ideas of all things that ought to be embraced in their instructions. These ideas are to be gained, either by contemplation upon the things themselves as they are presented naturally, or by the study of those books in which they are rationally and clearly explained. Nor will such study ever be irksome to him whose generous desire after knowledge, is thus deservedly gratified.

10. But it must be understood, that although scientific definitions are said to be *of things*, they are not copied immediately from the real essence of the things, but are formed from the conceptions of the author's mind concerning that essence. Hence, as Duncan justly remarks, "A mistaken idea never fails to occasion a mistake also in the definition." Hence, too, the common distinction of the logicians, between definitions of the *name* and definitions of the *thing*, seems to have little or no foundation. The former term they applied to those definitions which describe the objects of pure intellection, such as triangles, and other geometrical figures; the latter, to those which define objects actually existing in external nature. The mathematical definitions, so noted for their certainty and completeness, have been supposed to have some peculiar preëminence, as belonging to the former class. But, in fact the idea of a triangle exists as substantively in the mind, as that of a tree, if not indeed more so; and if I define these two objects, my description will, in either case, be equally a definition both of name and

of the thing; but in neither, is it copied from any thing else than that notion which I have conceived, of the common properties of all triangles or of all trees.

11. Infinitives, and some other terms not called nouns, may be taken abstractly or substantively, so as to admit of what may be considered a regular definition; thus the question, "What is it *to read?*" is nearly the same as, "What is *reading?*" "What is it *to be wise?*" is little different from, "What is *wisdom?*" and a true answer might be, in either case, a true definition. Nor are those mere translations or explanations of words, with which our dictionaries and vocabularies abound, to be dispensed with in teaching: they prepare the student to read various authors with facility, and furnish him with a better choice of terms, when he attempts to write. And in making such choice, let him remember, that as affectation of *hard* words makes composition ridiculous, so the affectation of *easy* and *common* ones may make it unmanly. But not to digress. With respect to grammar, we must sometimes content ourselves with such explications of its customary terms, as cannot claim to be perfect definitions; for the most common and familiar things are not always those which it is the most easy to define. When Dr. Johnson was asked, "What is *poetry?*" he replied, "Why, sir, it is easier to tell what it is not. We all know what *light* is: but it is not easy *to tell what it is.*"—*Boswell's Life of Johnson*, Vol. iii, p. 402. This was thought by the biographer to have been well and ingeniously said.

12. But whenever we encounter difficulties of this sort, it may be worth while to seek for their *cause*. If we find it, the understanding is no longer puzzled. Dr. Johnson seemed to his biographer, to show, by this ready answer, the acuteness of his wit and discernment. But did not the wit consist in adroitly excusing himself, by an illusory comparison? What analogy is there between the things which he compares? Of the difficulty of defining *poetry,* and the difficulty of defining *light,* the reasons are as different as are

the two things themselves, *poetry* and *light*. The former is something so various and complex that it is hard to distinguish its essence from its accidents; the latter presents an idea so perfectly simple and unique that all men conceive of it exactly in the same way, while none can show wherein it essentially consists. But is it true, that, "We all know *what light is*?" Is it not rather true, that we know nothing at all about it, but what it is just as easy to tell as to think? We know it is that reflexible medium which enables us to see; and this is definition enough for all but the natively blind, to whom no definition perhaps can ever convey an adequate notion of its use in respect to sight.

13. If a person cannot tell what a thing is, it is commonly considered to be a fair inference, that he does not know. Will any grammarian say, "I know well enough what the thing is, but I cannot tell?" Yet, taken upon this common principle, the authors of our English grammars, (if in framing their definitions they have not been grossly wanting to themselves in the exercise of their own art,) may be charged, I think, with great ignorance, or great indistinctness of apprehension; and that, too, in relation to many things among the very simplest elements of their science. For example: Is it not a disgrace to a man of letters, to be unable to tell accurately what a letter is? Yet to say, with Lowth, Murray, Churchill, and a hundred others of inferior name, that, "*A letter* is *the first principle* or *least part* of a word," is to utter what is neither good English nor true doctrine. The two articles *a* and *the* are here inconsistent with each other. "*A letter*" is *one* letter, *any* letter; but "*the first principle* of a word" is, surely, not one or any principle taken *indefinitely*. Equivocal as the phrase is, it must mean either *some particular principle*, or some particular *first* principle, of a word; and, taken either way, the assertion is false. For it is manifest, that in *no sense* can we affirm of *each* of the letters of a word, that it is "*the first principle*" of that word. Take, for instance, the word *man*. Is *m* the first principle of this word? You may answer, "Yes; for it is the first *letter*." Is *a* the first principle? "No; it is

the *second*." But *n* too is a letter; and is *n* the first principle? "No; it is the *last*!" This grammatical error might have been avoided by saying, "*Letters* are the first principles, or least parts, of words." But still the definition would not be true, nor would it answer the question, What is a letter? The true answer to which is: "A letter is an alphabetic *character*, which commonly represents some elementary sound of human articulation, or speech."

14. This true definition sufficiently distinguishes letters from the marks used in punctuation, because the latter are not alphabetic, and they represent silence, rather than sound; and also from the Arabic figures used for numbers, because these are no part of any alphabet, and they represent certain entire words, no one of which consists only of one letter, or of a single element of articulation. The same may be said of all the characters used for abbreviation; as, & for *and*, $ for *dollars*, or the marks peculiar to mathematicians, to astronomers, to druggists, &c. None of these are alphabetic, and they represent significant words, and not single elementary sounds: it would be great dullness, to assume that a word and an elementary sound are one and the same thing. But the reader will observe that this definition embraces *no idea* contained in the faulty one to which I am objecting; neither indeed could it, without a blunder. So wide from the mark is that notion of a letter, which the popularity of Dr. Lowth and his copyists has made a hundred-fold more common than any other![67] According to an other erroneous definition given by these same gentlemen, "*Words* are articulate *sounds*, used by common consent, as signs of our ideas."— *Murray's Gram.*, p. 22; *Kirkham's*, 20; *Ingersoll's*, 7; *Alger's*, 12; *Russell's*, 7; *Merchant's*, 9; *Fisk's*, 11; *Greenleaf's*, 20; and many others. See *Lowth's Gram.*, p. 6; from which almost all authors have taken the notion, that words consist of "*sounds*" only. But letters are no principles or parts of *sounds* at all; unless you will either have visible marks to be sounds, or the sign to be a principle or part of the thing signified. Nor are they always

principles or parts of *words*: we sometimes write what is *not a word*; as when, by letters, we denote pronunciation alone, or imitate brute voices. If words were formed of articulate sounds only, they could not exist in books, or be in any wise known to the deaf and dumb. These two primary definitions, then, are both false; and, taken together, they involve the absurdity of dividing things acknowledged to be indivisible. In utterance, we cannot divide consonants from their vowels; on paper, we can. Hence letters are the least parts of written language only; but the least parts of spoken words are syllables, and not letters. Every definition of a consonant implies this.

15. They who cannot define a letter or a word, may be expected to err in explaining other grammatical terms. In my opinion, nothing is well written, that can possibly be misunderstood; and if any definition be likely to *suggest* a wrong idea, this alone is enough to condemn it: nor does it justify the phraseology, to say, that a more reasonable construction can be put upon it. By Murray and others, the young learner is told, that, "A *vowel* is an articulate *sound*, that can be perfectly *uttered by itself*;" as if a vowel were nothing but a sound, and that a sort of echo, which can *utter itself*; and next, that, "A *consonant* is an articulate *sound*, which cannot be perfectly uttered *without the help of* a vowel." Now, by their own showing, every letter is either a vowel or a consonant; hence, according to these definitions, all the letters are articulate *sounds*. And, if so, what is a "silent letter?" It is a *silent articulate sound!* Again: ask a boy, "What is a *triphthong?*" He answers in the words of Murray, Weld, Pond, Smith, Adams, Kirkham, Merchant, Ingersoll, Bacon, Alger, Worcester, and others: "A triphthong is the union of three vowels, *pronounced in like manner*: as *eau* in beau, *iew* in view." He accurately cites an entire paragraph from his grammar, but does he well conceive how the three vowels in *beau* or *view* are "pronounced *in like manner?*" Again: "A *syllable* is a *sound*, either simple or *compound*, pronounced by a single impulse of the voice."—*Murray's Gram.*, 8vo, p.

22. This definition resolves syllables into *sounds*; whereas their true elements are *letters*. It also mistakes the participle *compounded* for the adjective *compound*; whereas the latter only is the true reverse of *simple*. A *compound sound* is a sound composed of others which may be separated; a *sound compounded* is properly that which is made an ingredient with others, but which may itself be simple.

16. It is observable, that in their attempts to explain these prime elements of grammar, Murray, and many others who have copied him, overlook all *written* language; whereas their very science itself took its origin, name, and nature, from the invention of writing; and has consequently no bearing upon any dialect which has not been written. Their definitions absurdly resolve letters, vowels, consonants, syllables, and words, all into *sounds*; as if none of these things had any existence on paper, or any significance to those who read in silence. Hence, their explanations of all these elements, as well as of many other things equally essential to the study, are palpably erroneous. I attribute this to the carelessness with which men have compiled or made up books of grammar; and that carelessness to those various circumstances, already described, which have left diligence in a grammarian no hope of praise or reward. Without alluding here to my own books, no one being obliged to accuse himself, I doubt whether we have any school grammar that is much less objectionable in this respect, than Murray's; and yet I am greatly mistaken, if nine tenths of all the definitions in Murray's system are not faulty. "It was this sort of definitions, which made *Scaliger* say, '*Nihil infelicius definitore grammatico.*'"—See *Johnson's Gram. Com.*, p. 351; also *Paragraph* 5th, above.

17. Nor can this objection be neutralized by saying, it is a mere matter of opinion—a mere prejudice originating in rivalry. For, though we have ample choice of terms, and may frequently assign to particular words a meaning and an explanation which are in some degree arbitrary; yet whenever we attempt to define things under the name which custom has positively fixed upon them, we are no longer left to arbitrary explications; but are bound to think and to say that only which shall commend itself to the understanding of others, as being altogether true to nature. When a word is well understood to denote a particular object or class of objects, the definition of it ought to be in strict conformity to what is known of the real being and properties of the thing or things contemplated. A definition of this kind is a proposition susceptible of proof and illustration; and therefore whatsoever is erroneously assumed to be the proper meaning of such a term, may be refuted. But those persons who take every thing upon trust, and choose both to learn and to teach mechanically, often become so slavishly habituated to the peculiar phraseology of their text-books, that, be the absurdity of a particular expression what it may, they can neither discover nor suspect any inaccuracy in it. It is also very natural even for minds more independent and acute, to regard with some reverence whatsoever was gravely impressed upon them in childhood. Hence the necessity that all school-books should proceed from skillful hands. Instruction should tell things as they are, and never falter through negligence.

18. I have admitted that definitions are not the only means by which a general knowledge of the import of language may be acquired; nor are they the only means by which the acquisition of such knowledge may be aided. To exhibit or point out *things* and tell their names, constitutes a large part of that instruction by which the meaning of words is conveyed to the young mind; and, in many cases, a mere change or apposition of terms may

sufficiently explain our idea. But when we would guard against the possibility of misapprehension, and show precisely what is meant by a word, we must fairly define it. There are, however, in every language, many words which do not admit of a formal definition. The import of all definitive and connecting particles must be learned from usage, translation, or derivation; and nature reserves to herself the power of explaining the objects of our simple original perceptions. "All words standing for complex ideas are definable; but those by which we denote simple ideas, are not. For the perceptions of this latter class, having no other entrance into the mind, than by sensation or reflection, can be acquired only by experience."— *Duncan's Logic*, p. 63. "And thus we see, that as our simple ideas are the materials and foundation of knowledge, so the names of simple ideas may be considered as the elementary parts of language, beyond which we cannot trace the meaning and signification of words. When we come to them, we suppose the ideas for which they stand to be already known; or, if they are not, experience alone must be consulted, and not definitions or explications."—*Ibid.*, p. 69.

19. But this is no apology for the defectiveness of any definition which might be made correct, or for the effectiveness of our English grammars, in the frequent omission of all explanation, and the more frequent adoption of some indirect form of expression. It is often much easier to make some loose observation upon what is meant by a given word or term in science, than to frame a faultless definition of the thing; because it is easier to refer to some of the relations, qualities, offices, or attributes of things, than to discern wherein their essence consists, so as to be able to tell directly and clearly what they are. The improvement of our grammatical code in this respect, was one of the principal objects which I thought it needful to attempt, when I first took up the pen as a grammarian. I cannot pretend to have seen, of course, every definition and rule which has been published on this subject; but, if I do not misjudge a service too humble for boasting, I

have myself framed a greater number of new or improved ones, than all other English grammarians together. And not a few of them have, since their first publication in 1823, been complimented to a place in other grammars than my own. This is in good keeping with the authorship which has been spoken of in an other chapter; but I am constrained to say, it affords no proof that they were well written. If it did, the definitions and rules in Murray's grammar must undoubtedly be thought the most correct that ever have been given: they have been more frequently copied than any others.

20. But I have ventured to suggest, that nine tenths of this author's definitions are bad, or at least susceptible of some amendment. If this can be shown to the satisfaction of the reader, will he hope to find an other English grammar in which the eye of criticism may not detect errors and deficiencies with the same ease? My object is, to enforce attention to the proprieties of speech; and this is the very purpose of all grammar. To exhibit here all Murray's definitions, with criticisms upon them, would detain us too long. We must therefore be content to take a part of them as a sample. And, not to be accused of fixing only upon the worst, we will take a *series*. Let us then consider in their order his definitions of the nine parts of speech;—for, calling the participle a verb, he reduces the sorts of words to that number. And though not one of his nine definitions now stands exactly as it did in his early editions, I think it may be said, that not one of them is now, if it ever has been, expressed grammatically.

21. FIRST DEFINITION:—"An Article is a word *prefixed* to substantives, *to point them out*, and to show how far their[68] signification extends."—*Murray, and others, from, Lowth's Gram.*, p. 10. This is obscure. In what manner, or in what respect, does an article point out substantives? To point them out *as such*, or to show which words are substantives, seems at first view to be the meaning intended; but it is said

soon after, "*A* or *an* is used in a vague sense, to *point out* one single *thing* of the kind, in other respects *indeterminate*; as, 'Give me *a* book;' 'Bring me *an* apple.'"—*Lowth*, p. 11; *Murray*, p. 31. And again: "It is *of the nature* of both the articles to determine or limit *the thing* spoken of."—*Murray's Gram.*, 8vo, p. 170. Now to point out *nouns* among the parts of speech, and to point out *things* as individuals of their class, are very different matters; and which of these is the purpose for which articles are used, according to Lowth and Murray? Their definition says the former, their explanations imply the latter; and I am unable to determine which they really meant. The term *placed before* would have been better than "*prefixed*;" because the latter commonly implies junction, as well as location. The word "*indeterminate*" is not a very easy one for a boy; and, when he has found out what it means, he may possibly not know to which of the four preceding nouns it ought to be referred:—"in a vague *sense*, to point out one single *thing* of the *kind*, in other *respects* indeterminate." What is this "vague sense?" and what is it, that is "indeterminate?"

22. SECOND DEFINITION:—"A Substantive or Noun is the name of any thing *that* exists, or of *which* we have any notion."—*Murray, and others*. According to his own syntax, this sentence of Murray's is wrong; for he himself suggests, that when two or more relative clauses refer to the same antecedent, the same pronoun should be used in each. Of clauses connected like these, this is true. He should therefore have said, "A Substantive, or Noun, is the name of any thing *which* exists, or of *which* we have any notion." His rule, however, though good against a text like this, is utterly wrong in regard to many others, and not very accurate in taking *two* for a "*series*" thus: "Whatever relative is used, in one of a *series* of clauses relating to the same antecedent, the same relative ought, generally to be used in *them all*. In the following sentence, *this rule is violated*: 'It is remarkable, that Holland, against *which* the war was undertaken, and *that*, in the very beginning, was reduced to the brink of destruction, lost nothing.'

The clause ought to have been, 'and *which* in the very beginning.'"—*Murray's Gram.*, 8vo, p. 155. But both the rule and the example, badly as they correspond, were borrowed from Priestley's Grammar, p. 102, where the text stands thus: "Whatever relative *be* used, in one of a *series* of clauses, relating to the same antecedent, the same ought to be used in *them all*. 'It is remarkable, that Holland,'" &c.

23. THIRD DEFINITION:—"An Adjective is a word added to a substantive, to express *its* quality."—*Lowth, Murray, Bullions, Pond, and others*. Here we have the choice of two meanings; but neither of them is according to truth. It seems doubtful whether "*its* quality" is the *adjective's* quality, or the *substantive's*; but in either sense, the phrase is false; for an adjective is added to a noun, not to express any quality either of the adjective or of the noun, but to express some quality of the *thing signified* by the noun. But the definition is too much restricted; for adjectives may be added to pronouns as well as to nouns, nor do they always express *quality*.

24. FOURTH DEFINITION:—"A Pronoun is a word used instead of a noun, to *avoid the too frequent* repetition of *the same word*."—*Dr. Ash's Gram.*, p. 25; *Murray's*, 28 and 50; *Felton's*, 18; *Alger's*, 13; *Bacon's*, 10; *and others*. The latter part of this sentence is needless, and also contains several errors. 1. The verb *avoid* is certainly very ill-chosen; because it implies intelligent agency, and not that which is merely instrumental. 2. The article *the* is misemployed for *a*; for, "*the* too frequent repetition," should mean *some particular* too frequent repetition—an idea not intended here, and in itself not far from absurdity. 3. The phrase, "*the same word*" may apply to the pronoun itself as well as to the noun: in saying, "*I* came, *I* saw, *I* conquered," there is as frequent a repetition of *the same word*, as in saying, "*Cæsar* came, *Cæsar* saw, *Cæsar* conquered." If, therefore, the latter part of this definition must be retained, the whole should be written

thus: "A Pronoun is a word used *in stead* of a noun, to *prevent* too frequent *a* repetition of *it*."

25. FIFTH DEFINITION:—"A Verb is a word which signifies *to be, to do*, or *to suffer*"—*Lowth, Murray, and others*. NOTE:—"A verb may generally be distinguished by *its making sense* with any of the personal pronouns, or the word *to* before it."—*Murray, and others*. It is confessedly difficult to give a perfect definition of a *verb*; and if, with Murray, we will have the participles to be verbs, there must be no small difficulty in forming one that shall be tolerable. Against the foregoing old explanation, it may be objected, that the phrase *to suffer*, being now understood in a more limited sense than formerly, does not well express the nature or import of a passive verb. I have said, "A Verb is a word that signifies *to be, to act*, or *to be acted upon*." Children cannot readily understand, how every thing that is in any way *acted upon*, may be said *to suffer*. The participle, I think, should be taken as a distinct part of speech, and have its own definition. The note added by Murray to his definition of a verb, would prove the participle not to be included in this part of speech, and thus practically contradict his scheme. It is also objectionable in respect to construction. The phrase "*by its making sense*" is at least very questionable English; for "*its making*" supposes *making* to be a noun, and "*making sense*" supposes it to be an active participle. But Lowth says, "Let it be either the one or the other, and abide by its own construction." Nay, the author himself, though he therein contradicts an other note of his own, virtually condemns the phrase, by his caution to the learner against treating words in *ing*, "as if they were of an *amphibious species*, partly nouns and partly verbs."—*Murray's Gram.*, 8vo, p. 193.

26. SIXTH DEFINITION:—"*An* Adverb is *a part of speech joined* to a verb, an adjective, *and sometimes to* another adverb, to express some *quality* or *circumstance* respecting *it*."—*Murray's Gram.*, pp. 28 and 114.

See *Dr. Ash's Gram.*, p. 47. This definition contains many errors; some of which are gross blunders. 1. The first word, "*An,*" is erroneously put for *The: an* adverb is *one* adverb, not the whole class; and, if, "*An* adverb is a part of speech," any and every adverb is a *part of speech*; then, how many parts of speech are there? 2. The word "*joined*" is not well chosen; for, with the exception of *not* in *cannot,* the adverb is very rarely *joined* to the word to which it relates. 3. The want of a comma before *joined,* perverts the construction; for the phrase, "*speech joined* to a verb," is nonsense; and to suppose *joined* to relate to the noun *part,* is not much better. 4. The word "*and*" should be *or*; because no adverb is ever added to three or four different terms at once. 5. The word "*sometimes*" should be omitted; because it is needless, and because it is inconsistent with the only conjunction which will make the definition true. 6. The preposition "*to*" should either be inserted before "*an adjective,*" or suppressed before the term which follows; for when several words occur in the same construction, uniformity of expression is desirable. 7. For the same reason, (if custom may be thus far conformed to analogy,) the article "*an*" ought, in cases like this, if not always, to be separated from the word *other*; thus, "An adverb is a word added to *a* verb, *a* participle, *an* adjective, or *an* other adverb." Were the eye not familiar with it, *another* would be thought as irregular as *theother*. 8. The word "*quality*" is wrong; for no adverb ever expresses any *quality,* as such; qualities are expressed by *adjectives,* and never, in any direct manner, by adverbs. 9. The "*circumstances*" which we express by adverbs never belong to the *words,* as this definition avers that they do, but always to the *actions* or *qualities* which the words signify. 10. The pronoun *it,* according to Murray's second rule of syntax, ought to be *them,* and so it stands in his own early editions; but if *and* be changed to *or,* as I have said it should be, the pronoun *it* will be right.

27. SEVENTH DEFINITION:—"Prepositions serve to connect words with *one another,* and to show the relation *between them.*"—*Lowth,*

Murray, and others. This is only an observation, not a definition, as it ought to have been; nor does it at all distinguish the preposition from the conjunction. It does not reach the thing in question. Besides, it contains an actual solecism in the expression. The word "*between*" implies but *two* things; and the phrase "*one another*" is not applicable where there are but two. It should be, "to connect words with *each other*, and to show the *relation between* them;"—or else, "to connect words with *one an other*, and to show the *relations among* them." But the latter mode of expression would not apply to prepositions considered severally, but only to the whole class.

28. EIGHTH DEFINITION:—"A Conjunction is *a part of speech* that is *chiefly* used to connect sentences; so as, out of two *or more* sentences, to make but one: it sometimes connects only words."—*Murray, and others*. Here are more than thirty words, awkwardly and loosely strung together; and all that is said in them, might be much better expressed in half the number. For example: "A Conjunction is a word which connects other terms, and commonly of two sentences makes but one." But verbosity and want of unity are not the worst faults of this definition. We have three others to point out. 1. "A conjunction is" not "*a part of speech*;" because *a* conjunction is *one* conjunction, and a part of speech is a whole class, or sort, of words. A similar error was noticed in Murray's definition of an adverb; and so common has this blunder become, that by a comparison of the definitions which different authors have given of the parts of speech, probably it will be found, that, by some hand or other, every one of the ten has been commenced in this way. 2. The words "*or more*" are erroneous, and ought to be omitted; for no one conjunction can connect more than two terms, in that consecutive order which the sense requires. Three or more simple sentences may indeed form a compound sentence; but, as they cannot be joined in a *cluster*, they must have two or more connectives. 3. The last clause erroneously suggests, that any or every conjunction

"*sometimes connects only words*;" but the conjunctions which may connect only words, are not more than five, whereas those which connect only sentences are four times as many.

29. NINTH DEFINITION:—"Interjections are words *thrown in between the parts of a sentence*, to express the passions or emotions of the *speaker*; as, 'O Virtue! how amiable thou art!'"—*Murray, and many others*. This definition, which has been copied from grammar to grammar, and committed to memory millions of times, is obviously erroneous, and directly contradicted by the example. Interjections, though often enough thrown in between the parts of a *discourse*, are very rarely "thrown in between the parts of a *sentence*." They more frequently occur at the beginning of a sentence than any where else; and, in such cases, they do not come under this narrow definition. The author, at the head of his chapter on interjections, appends to this definition two other examples; both of which contradict it in like manner: "*Oh*! I have alienated my friend."—"*Alas*! I fear for life." Again: Interjections are used occasionally, in *written*, as well as in *oral* discourse; nor are they less indicative of the emotions of the *writer*, than of those "of the *speaker*."

30. I have thus exhibited, with all intentional fairness of criticism, the entire series of these nine primary definitions; and the reader may judge whether they sustain the praises which have been bestowed on the book, [69] or confirm the allegations which I have made against it. He will understand that my design is, here, as well as in the body of this work, to teach grammar practically, by *rectifying*, so far as I may, all sorts of mistakes either in it or respecting it; to compose a book which, by a condensed exposition of such errors as are commonly found in other grammars, will at once show the need we have of a better, and be itself a fit substitute for the principal treatises which it censures. Grammatical errors are universally considered to be small game for critics. They must therefore

be very closely grouped together, to be worth their room in this work. Of the tens of thousands who have learned for grammar a multitude of ungrammatical definitions and rules, comparatively few will ever know what I have to say of their acquisitions. But this I cannot help. To the readers of the present volume it is due, that its averments should be clearly illustrated by particular examples; and it is reasonable that these should be taken from the most accredited sources, whether they do honour to their framers or not. My argument is only made so much the stronger, as the works which furnish its proofs, are the more esteemed, the more praised, or the more overrated.

31. Murray tells us, "There is no necessary connexion between words and ideas."—*Octavo Gram.*, Vol. i, p. 139. Though this, as I before observed, is not altogether true, he doubtless had very good reason to distinguish, in his teaching, "between *the sign* and *the thing signified*." Yet, in his own definitions and explanations, he frequently *confounds* these very things which he declares to be so widely different as not even to have a "necessary connexion." Errors of this kind are very common in all our English grammars. Two instances occur in the following sentence; which also contains an error in doctrine, and is moreover obscure, or rather, in its literal sense, palpably absurd: "To substantives belong gender, number, and case; and *they* are *all of* the third person *when spoken of*, and of the second person *when spoken to*."—*Murray's Gram.*, p. 38; *Alger's Murray*, 16; *Merchant's*, 23; *Bacon's*, 12; *Maltby's*, 12; *Lyon's*, 7; *Guy's*, 4; *Ingersoll's*, 26; *S. Putnam's*, 13; *T. H. Miller's*, 17; *Rev. T. Smith's*, 13. Who, but a child taught by language like this, would ever think of *speaking to a noun*? or, that a noun of the second person *could not be spoken of*? or, that a noun cannot be put in the *first person*, so as to agree with *I* or *we*? Murray himself once taught, that, "Pronouns *must always agree* with their antecedents, *and* the nouns for which they stand, in gender, number, and *person*;" and he departed from a true and important principle of syntax,

when he altered his rule to its present form. But I have said that the sentence above is obscure, or its meaning absurd. What does the pronoun "*they*" represent? "*Substantives*," according to the author's intent; but "*gender, number,* and *case,*" according to the obvious construction of the words. Let us try a parallel:" To scriveners belong pen, ink, and paper; and *they* are all of primary importance when there is occasion to use them, and of none at all when they are not needed." Now, if this sentence is *obscure,* the other is not less so; but, if this is perfectly *clear,* so that what is said is obviously and only what is intended, then it is equally clear, that what is said in the former, is gross absurdity, and that the words cannot reasonably be construed into the sense which the writer, and his copyists, designed.

32. All Murray's grammars, not excepting the two volumes octavo, are as *incomplete* as they are *inaccurate*; being deficient in many things which are of so great importance that they should not be excluded from the very smallest epitome. For example: On the subject of the *numbers,* he attempted but one definition, and that is a fourfold solecism. Ho speaks of the *persons,* but gives neither definitions nor explanations. In treating of the *genders,* he gives but one formal definition. His section on the *cases* contains no regular definition. On the *comparison* of adjectives, and on the *moods* and *tenses* of verbs, he is also satisfied with a very loose mode of teaching. The work as a whole exhibits more industry than literary taste, more benevolence of heart than distinctness of apprehension; and, like all its kindred and progeny, fails to give to the principles of grammar that degree of clearness of which they are easily susceptible. The student does not know this, but he feels the effects of it, in the obscurity of his own views on the subject, and in the conscious uncertainty with which he applies those principles. In grammar, the terms *person, number, gender, case, mood, tense,* and many others, are used in a technical and peculiar sense; and, in all scientific works, the sense of technical terms should be clearly and precisely defined. Nothing can be gained by substituting other names of modern invention; for these also

would need definitions as much as the old. We want to know the things themselves, and what they are most appropriately called. We want a book which will tell us, in proper order, and in the plainest manner, what all the elements of the science are.

33. What does he know of grammar, who cannot directly and properly answer such questions as these?—"What are numbers, in grammar? What is the singular number? What is the plural number? What are persons, in grammar? What is the first person? What is the second person? What is the third person? What are genders, in grammar? What is the masculine gender? What is the feminine gender? What is the neuter gender? What are cases, in grammar? What is the nominative case? What is the possessive case? What is the objective case?"—And yet the most complete acquaintance with every sentence or word of Murray's tedious compilation, may leave the student at a loss for a proper answer, not only to each of these questions, but also to many others equally simple and elementary! A boy may learn by heart all that Murray ever published on the subject of grammar, and still be left to confound the numbers in grammar with numbers in arithmetic, or the persons in grammar with persons in civil life! Nay, there are among the professed *improvers* of this system of grammar, *men* who have actually confounded these things, which are so totally different in their natures! In "Smith's New Grammar on the Productive System," a work in which Murray is largely copied and strangely metamorphosed, there is an abundance of such confusion. For instance: "What is the meaning of the word *number*? Number means *a sum that may be counted.*"—*R. C. Smith's New Gram.*, p. 7. From this, by a tissue of half a dozen similar absurdities, called *inductions*, the novice is brought to the conclusion that the numbers are *two*—as if there were in nature but two sums that might be counted! There is no end to the sickening detail of such blunders. How many grammars tell us, that, "The first person is the *person who speaks*;" that, "The second person is the *person spoken to*;" and that,

"the third person is the *person spoken of*!" As if the three persons of a verb, or other part of speech, were so many *intelligent beings*! As if, by exhibiting a word in the three persons, (as *go, goest, goes*,) we put it first *into the speaker*, then *into the hearer*, and then *into somebody else*! Nothing can be more abhorrent to grammar, or to sense, than such confusion. The things which are identified in each of these three definitions, are as unlike as Socrates and moonshine! The one is a thinking being; the other, a mere form peculiar to certain words. But Chandler, of Philadelphia, ("the Grammar King," forsooth!) without mistaking the grammatical persons for rational souls, has contrived to crowd into his definition of *person* more errors of conception and of language,—more insult to common sense,— than one could have believed it possible to put together in such space. And this ridiculous old twaddle, after six and twenty years, he has deliberately re-written and lately republished as something "adapted to the schools of America." It stands thus: "*Person is a distinction which is made in a noun between its representation of its object, either as spoken to, or spoken of.*"— Chandler's E. Grammar; Edition of 1821, p. 16; Ed. 1847, p. 21.

34. Grammarians have often failed in their definitions, because it is impossible to define certain terms in the way in which the description has been commonly attempted. He who undertakes what is impossible must necessarily fail; and fail too, to the discredit of his ingenuity. It is manifest that whenever a generic name in the singular number is to be defined, the definition must be founded upon some property or properties common to all the particular things included under the term. Thus, if I would define a *globe*, a *wheel*, or a *pyramid*, my description must be taken, not from what is peculiar to one or an other of these things, but from those properties only which are common to all globes, all wheels, or all pyramids. But what property has *unity* in common with *plurality*, on which a definition of *number* may be founded? What common property have the *three cases*, by which we can clearly define *case*? What have the *three persons* in common,

which, in a definition of *person,* could be made evident to a child? Thus all the great classes of grammatical modifications, namely, *persons, numbers, genders, cases, moods,* and *tenses,* though they admit of easy, accurate, and obvious definitions in the plural, can scarcely be defined at all in the singular. I do not say, that the terms *person, number, gender, case, mood,* and *tense,* ia their technical application to grammar, are all of them equally and absolutely undefinable in the singular; but I say, that no definition, just in sense and suitable for a child, can ever be framed for any one of them. Among the thousand varied attempts of grammarians to explain them so, there are a hundred gross solecisms for every tolerable definition. For this, as I have shown, there is a very simple reason in the nature of the things.

35. But this reason, as well as many other truths equally important and equally clear, our common grammarians, have, so far as I know, every man of them, overlooked. Consequently, even when they were aiming at the right thing, they frequently fell into gross errors of expression; and, what is still more surprising, such errors have been entailed upon the very art of grammar, and the art of authorship itself, by the prevalence of an absurd notion, that modern writers on this subject can be meritorious authors without originality. Hence many a school-boy is daily rehearsing from his grammar-book what he might well be ashamed to have written. For example, the following definition from Murray's grammar, is found in perhaps a dozen other compends, all professing to teach the art of speaking and writing with propriety: "*Number* is the *consideration of an object,* as *one* or *more.*" [70] Yet this short sentence, as I have before suggested, is a fourfold solecism. *First,* the word "*number*" is wrong; because those modifications of language, which distinguish unity and plurality, cannot be jointly signified by it. *Secondly,* the word "*consideration*" is wrong; because *number* is not *consideration,* in any sense which can be put upon the terms: *condition, constitution, configuration,* or any other word beginning with *con,* would have done just as well. *Thirdly,* "the consideration of *an* object

as *one,*" is but idle waste of thought; for, that one thing is one,—that *an* object is *one* object,—every child knows by *intuition,* and not by "*consideration.*" *Lastly,* to consider "*an* object as *more*" than one, is impossible; unless this admirable definition lead us into a misconception in so plain a case! So much for the art of "the grammatical definer."

36. Many other examples, equally faulty and equally common, might, be quoted and criticised for the further proof and illustration of what I have alleged. But the reader will perhaps judge the foregoing to be sufficient. I have wished to be brief, and yet to give my arguments, and the neglected facts upon which they rest, their proper force upon the mind. Against such prejudices as may possibly arise from the authorship of rival publications, or from any interest in the success of one book rather than of an other, let both my judges and me be on our guard. I have intended to be fair; for captiousness is not criticism. If the reader perceives in these strictures any improper bias, he has a sort of discernment which it is my misfortune to lack. Against the compilers of grammars, I urge no conclusions at which any man can hesitate, who accedes to my preliminary remarks upon them; and these may be summed up in the following couplet of the poet Churchill:

"To copy beauties, forfeits all pretence
To fame;—to copy faults, is want of sense."

BRIEF NOTICES OF THE SCHEMES OF CERTAIN GRAMMARS.

"Sed ut perveniri ad summa nisi ex principiis non potest: ita, procedente jam opere, minima incipiunt esse quæ prima sunt."—QUINTILIAN. *De Inst. Orat.,* Lib. x, Cap. 1, p. 560.

1. The *history* of grammar, in the proper sense of the term, has heretofore been made no part of the study. I have imagined that many of its details might be profitable, not only to teachers, but to that class of learners for whose use this work is designed. Accordingly, in the preceding pages, there have been stated numerous facts properly historical, relating either to particular grammars, or to the changes and progress of this branch of instruction. These various details it is hoped will be more entertaining, and perhaps for that reason not less useful, than those explanations which belong merely to the construction and resolution of sentences. The attentive reader must have gathered from the foregoing chapters some idea of what the science owes to many individuals whose names are connected with it. But it seems proper to devote to this subject a few pages more, in order to give some further account of the origin and character of certain books.

2. The manuals by which grammar was first taught in English, were not properly English Grammars. They were translations of the Latin Accidence; and were designed to aid British youth in acquiring a knowledge of the Latin language, rather than accuracy in the use of their own. The two languages were often combined in one book, for the purpose of teaching sometimes both together, and sometimes one through the medium of the other. The study of such works doubtless had a tendency to modify, and perhaps at that time to improve, the English style of those who used them. For not only must variety of knowledge have led to copiousness of expression, but the most cultivated minds would naturally be most apt to observe what was orderly in the use of speech. A language, indeed, after its proper form is well fixed by letters, must resist all introduction of foreign idioms, or become corrupted. Hence it is, that Dr. Johnson avers, "The great pest of speech is frequency of translation. No book was ever turned from one language into another, without imparting something of its native idiom; this is the most mischievous and comprehensive innovation."—*Preface to Joh. Dict.,* 4to, p. 14. Without expressly controverting this opinion, or

offering any justification of mere metaphrases, or literal translations, we may well assert, that the practice of comparing different languages, and seeking the most appropriate terms for a free version of what is ably written, is an exercise admirably calculated to familiarize and extend grammatical knowledge.

3. Of the class of books here referrred [sic—KTH] to, that which I have mentioned in an other chapter, as Lily's or King Henry's Grammar, has been by far the most celebrated and the most influential. Concerning this treatise, it is stated, that its parts were not put together in the present form, until eighteen or twenty years after Lily's death. "The time when this work was completed," says the preface of 1793, "has been differently related by writers. Thomas Hayne places it in the year 1543, and Anthony Wood, in 1545. But neither of these accounts can be right; for I have seen a beautiful copy, printed upon vellum, and illuminated, anno 1542, in quarto. And it may be doubted whether this was the first edition."—*John Ward, Pref.*, p. vii. In an Introductory Lecture, read before the University of London in 1828, by Thomas Dale, professor of English literature, I find the following statement: "In this reign,"—the reign of Henry VIII,—"the study of grammar was reduced to a system, by the promulgation of many grammatical treatises; one of which was esteemed of sufficient importance to be honoured with a royal name. It was called, 'The Grammar of King Henry the Eighth;' and to this, 'with other works, the young Shakspeare was probably indebted for some learning and much loyalty.' But the honour of producing the first English grammar is claimed by William Bullokar, who published, in the year 1586, 'A Bref Grammar for English,' being, to use his own words, 'the first Grammar for English that ever waz, except my Grammar at large.'"

4. Ward's preface to Lily commences thus: "If we look back to the origin of our common *Latin Grammar,* we shall find it was no hasty performance,

nor the work of a single person; but composed at different times by several eminent and learned men, till the whole was at length finished, and by the order of *King Henry* VIII.[,] brought into that form in which it has ever since continued. The *English introduction* was written by the reverend and learned Dr. *John Colet*, Dean of St. *Paul's*, for the use of the school he had lately founded there; and was dedicated by him to *William Lily*, the first high master of that school, in the year 1510; for which reason it has usually gone by the name of *Paul's Accidence*. The substance of it remains the same, as at first; though it has been much altered in the manner of expression, and sometimes the order, with other improvements. The *English syntax* was the work of *Lily*, as appears by the title in the most ancient editions, which runs thus: *Gulielmi Lilii Angli Rudimenta*. But it has been greatly improved since his time, both with, regard to the method, and an enlargement of double the quantity."

5. Paul's Accidence is therefore probably the oldest grammar that can now be found in our language. It is not, however, an English grammar; because, though written in antique English, and embracing many things which are as true of our language as of any other, it was particularly designed for the teaching of *Latin*. It begins thus: "In speech be these eight parts following: Noun, Pronoun, Verb, Participle, declined; Adverb, Conjunction, Preposition, Interjection, undeclined." This is the old platform of the Latin grammarians; which differs from that of the Greek grammars, only in having no Article, and in separating the Interjection from the class of Adverbs. Some Greek grammarians, however, separate the Adjective from the Noun, and include the Participle with the Verb: thus, "There are in Greek eight species of words, called Parts of Speech; viz. Article, Noun, Adjective, Pronoun, Verb, Adverb, Preposition, and Conjunction."—*Anthon's Valpy*, p. 18. With respect to our language, the plan of the Latin Accidence is manifestly inaccurate; nor can it be applied, without some variation, to the Greek. In both, as well as in all other languages that have

Articles, the best amendment of it, and the nearest adherence to it, is, to make the Parts of Speech *ten*; namely, the Article, the Noun, the Adjective, the Pronoun, the Verb, the Participle, the Adverb, the Conjunction, the Preposition, and the Interjection.

6. The best Latin grammarians admit that the Adjective ought not to be called a Noun; and the best Greek grammarians, that the Interjections ought not to be included among Adverbs. With respect to Participles, a vast majority of grammarians in general, make them a distinct species, or part of speech; but, on this point, the English grammarians are about equally divided: nearly one half include them with the verbs, and a few call them adjectives. In grammar, it is wrong to deviate from the old groundwork, except for the sake of truth and improvement; and, in this case, to vary the series of parts, by suppressing one and substituting an other, is in fact a greater innovation, than to make the terms ten, by adding one and dividing an other. But our men of nine parts of speech innovated yet more: they added the Article, as did the Greeks; divided the Noun into Substantive and Adjective; and, without good reason, suppressed the Participle. And, of latter time, not a few have thrown the whole into confusion, to show the world "the order of [their] understanding." What was grammar fifty years ago, some of these have not thought it worth their while to inquire! And the reader has seen, that, after all this, they can complacently talk of "the censure so frequently and so justly awarded to *unfortunate innovators*."— KIRKHAM'S *Gram.*, p. 10.

7. The old scheme of the Latin grammarians has seldom, if ever, been *literally* followed in English; because its distribution of the parts of speech, as declined and undeclined, would not be true with respect to the English participle. With the omission of this unimportant distinction, it was, however, scrupulously retained by Dilworth, by the author of the British Grammar, by William Ward, by Buchanan, and by some others now little

known, who chose to include both the article and the adjective with the noun, rather than to increase the number of the parts of speech beyond eight. Dr. Priestley says, "I shall adopt the *usual distribution* of words into eight classes; viz. Nouns, Adjectives, Pronouns, Verbs, Adverbs, Prepositions, Conjunctions, and Interjections.[71] I do this in compliance with the practice of most Grammarians; and because, *if any number, in a thing so arbitrary, must be fixed upon*, this seems to be as comprehensive and distinct as any. All the innovation I have made hath been to throw out the *Participle*, and substitute the *Adjective*, as more evidently a distinct part of speech."—*Rudiments of English Gram.*, p. 3. All this comports well enough with Dr. Priestley's haste and carelessness; but it is not true, that he either adopted, "the usual distribution of words," or made an other "as comprehensive and distinct as any." His "*innovation*," too, which has since been countenanced by many other writers, I have already shown to be greater, than if, by a promotion of the article and the adjective, he had made the parts of speech ten. Dr. Beattie, who was Priestley's coeval, and a much better scholar, adopted this number without hesitation, and called every one of them by what is still its right name: "In English there are *ten* sorts of words, which are all found in the following short sentence; 'I now see the good man coming; but, alas! he walks with difficulty.' *I* and *he* are pronouns; *now* is an adverb; *see* and *walks* are verbs; *the* is an article; *good*, an adjective; *man* and *difficulty* are nouns, the former substantive, the latter abstract; *coming* is a participle; *but*, a conjunction; *alas!* an interjection; *with*, a preposition. That no other sorts of words are necessary in language, will appear, when we have seen in what respects these are necessary."—*Beattie's Moral Science*, Vol. i, p. 30. This distribution is precisely that which the best *French* grammarians have *usually* adopted.

8. Dr. Johnson professes to adopt the division, the order, and the terms, "of the common grammarians, without inquiring whether a fitter distribution might not be found."—*Gram. before 4to Dict.*, p. 1. But, in the

Etymology of his Grammar, he makes no enumeration of the parts of speech, and treats only of articles, nouns, adjectives, pronouns, and verbs; to which if we add the others, according to the common grammarians, or according to his own Dictionary, the number will be *ten*. And this distribution, which was adopted by Dr. Ash about 1765, by Murray the schoolmaster about 1790, by Caleb Alexander in 1795, and approved by Dr. Adam in 1793, has since been very extensively followed; as may be seen in Dr. Crombie's treatise, in the Rev. Matt. Harrison's, in Dr. Mandeville's reading-books, and in the grammars of Harrison, Staniford, Alden, Coar, John Peirce, E. Devis, C. Adams, D. Adams, Chandler, Comly, Jaudon, Ingersoll, Hull, Fuller, Greenleaf, Kirkham, Ferd. H. Miller, Merchant, Mack, Nutting, Bucke, Beck, Barrett, Barnard, Maunder, Webber, Emmons, Hazen, Bingham, Sanders, and many others. Dr. Lowth's distribution is the same, except that he placed the adjective after the pronoun, the conjunction after the preposition, and, like Priestley, called the participle a verb, thus making the parts of speech *nine*. He also has been followed by many; among whom are Bicknell, Burn, Lennie, Mennye, Lindley Murray, W. Allen, Guy, Churchill, Wilson, Cobbett, Davis, David Blair, Davenport, Mendenhall, Wilcox, Picket, Pond, Russell, Bacon, Bullions, Brace, Hart, Lyon, Tob. H. Miller, Alger, A. Flint, Folker, S. Putnam, Cooper, Frost, Goldsbury, Hamlin, T. Smith, R. C. Smith, and Woodworth. But a third part of these, and as many more in the preceding list, are confessedly mere modifiers of Murray's compilation; and perhaps, in such a case, those have done best who have deviated least from the track of him whom they professed to follow.[72]

9. Some seem to have supposed, that by reducing the number of the parts of speech, and of the rules for their construction, the study of grammar would be rendered more easy and more profitable to the learner. But this, as would appear from the history of the science, is a mere retrogression towards the rudeness of its earlier stages. It is hardly worth while to dispute,

whether there shall be nine parts of speech or ten; and perhaps enough has already been stated, to establish the expediency of assuming the latter number. Every word in the language must be included in some class, and nothing is gained by making the classes larger and less numerous. In all the artificial arrangements of science, distinctions are to be made according to the differences in things; and the simple question here is, what differences among words shall be at first regarded. To overlook, in our primary division, the difference between a verb and a participle, is merely to reserve for a subdivision, or subsequent explanation, a species of words which most grammarians have recognized as a distinct sort in their original classification.

10. It should be observed that the early period of grammatical science was far remote from the days in which *English* grammar originated. Many things which we now teach and defend as grammar, were taught and defended two thousand years ago, by the philosophers of Greece and Rome. Of the parts of speech, Quintilian, who lived in the first century of our era, gives the following account: "For the ancients, among whom were Aristotle[73] and Theodectes, treated only of verbs, nouns, and conjunctions: as the verb is what we say, and the noun, that of which we say it, they judged the power of discourse to be in *verbs*, and the matter in *nouns*, but the connexion in *conjunctions*. Little by little, the philosophers, and especially the Stoics, increased the number: first, to the conjunctions were added *articles*; afterwards, *prepositions*; to nouns, was added the *appellation*; then the *pronoun*; afterwards, as belonging to each verb, the *participle*; and, to verbs in common, *adverbs*. Our language [i. e., the *Latin*] does not require articles, wherefore they are scattered among the other parts of speech; but there is added to the foregoing the *interjection*. But some, on the authority of good authors, make the parts only eight; as Aristarchus, and, in our day, Palæmon; who have included the vocable, or appellation, with the noun, as a species of it. But they who make the noun one and the

vocable an other, reckon nine. But there are also some who divide the vocable from the appellation; making the former to signify any thing manifest to sight or touch, as *house, bed*; and the latter, any thing to which either or both are wanting, as *wind, heaven, god, virtue*. They have also added the *asseveration* and the *attrectation*, which I do not approve. Whether the vocable or appellation should be included with the noun or not, as it is a matter of little consequence, I leave to the decision of others."— See QUINTIL. *de Inst. Orat.*, Lib. i, Cap. 4, §24.

11. Several writers on English grammar, indulging a strange unsettlement of plan, seem not to have determined in their own minds, how many parts of speech there are, or ought to be. Among these are Horne Tooke, Webster, Dalton, Cardell, Green, and Cobb; and perhaps, from what he says above, we may add the name of Priestley. The present disputation about the sorts of words, has been chiefly owing to the writings of Horne Tooke, who explains the minor parts of speech as mere abbreviations, and rejects, with needless acrimony, the common classification. But many have mistaken the nature of his instructions, no less than that of the common grammarians. This author, in his third chapter, supposes his auditor to say, "But you have not all this while informed me *how many parts of speech* you mean to lay down." To whom he replies, "That shall be as you please. Either *two*, or *twenty*, or *more*." Such looseness comported well enough with his particular purpose; because he meant to teach the derivation of words, and not to meddle at all with their construction. But who does not see that it is impossible to lay down rules for the *construction* of words, without first dividing them into the classes to which such rules apply? For example: if a man means to teach, that, "A verb must agree with its subject, or nominative, in person and number," must he not first show the learner *what words are verbs?* and ought he not to see in this rule a reason for not calling the participle a verb? Let the careless followers of Lowth and Priestley answer. Tooke did not care to preserve any parts of speech at all. His work

is not a system of grammar; nor can it be made the basis of any regular scheme of grammatical instruction. He who will not grant that the same words may possibly be used as different parts of speech, must make his parts of speech either very few or very many. This author says, "I do not allow that *any* words change their nature in this manner, so as to belong sometimes to one part of speech, and sometimes to another, from the different ways of using them. I never could perceive any such fluctuation in any word whatever."—*Diversions of Purley*, Vol. i, p. 68.

12. From his own positive language, I imagine this ingenious author never well considered what constitutes the sameness of words, or wherein lies the difference of the parts of speech; and, without understanding these things, a grammarian cannot but fall into errors, unless he will follow somebody that knows them. But Tooke confessedly contradicts, and outfaces "*all other Grammarians*" in the passage just cited. Yet it is plain, that the whole science of grammar—or at least the whole of etymology and syntax, which are its two principal parts—is based upon a division of words into the parts of speech; a division which necessarily refers, in many instances, the same words to different sections according to the manner in which they are used. "Certains mots répondent, ainsi au même temps, à diverses parties d'oraison selon que la grammaire les emploie diversement."—*Buffier*, Art. 150. "Some words, from the different ways in which they are used, belong sometimes to one part of speech, sometimes to another."—*M'Culloch's Gram.*, p. 37. "And so say all other Grammarians."—*Tooke, as above*.

13. The history of *Dr. Webster*, as a grammarian, is singular. He is remarkable for his changeableness, yet always positive; for his inconsistency, yet very learned; for his zeal "to correct popular errors," yet often himself erroneous; for his fertility in resources, yet sometimes meagre; for his success as an author, yet never satisfied; for his boldness of

innovation, yet fond of appealing to antiquity. His grammars are the least judicious, and at present the least popular, of his works. They consist of four or five different treatises, which for their mutual credit should never be compared: it is impossible to place any firm reliance upon the authority of a man who contradicts himself so much. Those who imagine that the last opinions of so learned a man must needs be right, will do well to wait, and see what will be his last: they cannot otherwise know to what his instructions will finally lead: Experience has already taught him the folly of many of his pretended improvements, and it is probable his last opinions of English grammar will be most conformable to that just authority with which he has ever been tampering. I do not say that he has not exhibited ingenuity as well as learning, or that he is always wrong when he contradicts a majority of the English grammarians; but I may venture to say, he was wrong when he undertook to disturb the common scheme of the parts of speech, as well as when he resolved to spell all words exactly as they are pronounced.

14. It is not commonly known with how rash a hand this celebrated author has sometimes touched the most settled usages of our language. In 1790, which was seven years after the appearance of his first grammar, he published an octavo volume of more than four hundred pages, consisting of Essays, moral, historical, political, and literary, which might have done him credit, had he not spoiled his book by a grammatical whim about the reformation of orthography. Not perceiving that English literature, multiplied as it had been within two or three centuries, had acquired a stability in some degree corresponding to its growth, he foolishly imagined it was still as susceptible of change and improvement as in the days of its infancy. Let the reader pardon the length of this digression, if for the sake of any future schemer who may chance to adopt a similar conceit, I cite from the preface to this volume a specimen of the author's practice and reasoning. The ingenious attorney had the good sense quickly to abandon this project,

and content himself with less glaring innovations; else he had never stood as he now does, in the estimation of the public. But there is the more need to record the example, because in one of the southern states the experiment has recently been tried again. A still abler member of the same profession, has renewed it but lately; and it is said there are yet remaining some converts to this notion of improvement. I copy literally, leaving all my readers and his to guess for themselves why he spelled "*writers*" with a *w* and "*riting*" without.

15. "During the course of ten or twelv yeers, I hav been laboring to correct popular errors, and to assist my yung brethren in the road to truth and virtue; my publications for theze purposes hav been numerous; much time haz been spent, which I do not regret, and much censure incurred, which my hart tells me I do not dezerv." * * * "The reeder wil observ that the *orthography* of the volum iz not uniform. The reezon iz, that many of the essays hav been published before, in the common orthography, and it would hav been a laborious task to copy the whole, for the sake of changing the spelling. In the essays, ritten within the last yeer, a considerable change of spelling iz introduced by way of experiment. This liberty waz taken by the writers before the age of queen Elizabeth, and to this we are indeted for the preference of modern spelling over that of Gower and Chaucer. The man who admits that the change of *hoasbonde, mynde, ygone, moneth* into *husband, mind, gone, month*, iz an improovment, must acknowlege also the riting of *helth, breth, rong, tung, munth*, to be an improovment. There iz no alternativ. Every possible reezon that could ever be offered for altering the spelling of wurds, stil exists in full force; and if a gradual reform should not be made in our language, it wil proov that we are less under the influence of reezon than our ancestors."—*Noah Webster's Essays, Preface*, p. xi.

16. But let us return, with our author, to the question of the parts of speech. I have shown that if we do not mean to adopt some less convenient

scheme, we must count them *ten*, and preserve their ancient order as well as their ancient names.[74] And, after all his vacillation in consequence of reading Horne Tooke, it would not be strange if Dr. Webster should come at last to the same conclusion. He was not very far from it in 1828, as may be shown by his own testimony, which he then took occasion to record. I will give his own words on the point: "There is great difficulty in devising a correct classification of the several sorts of words; and probably no classification that shall be simple and at the same time philosophically correct, can be invented. There are some words that do not strictly fall under any description of any class yet devised. Many attempts have been made and are still making to remedy this evil; but such schemes as I have seen, do not, in my apprehension, correct the defects of the old schemes, nor simplify the subject. On the other hand, all that I have seen, serve only to obscure and embarrass the subject, by substituting new arrangements and new terms which are as incorrect as the old ones, and less intelligible. I have attentively viewed these subjects, in all the lights which my opportunities have afforded, and am convinced that the distribution of words, most generally received, *is the best that can be formed*, with some slight alterations adapted to the particular construction of the English language."

17. This passage is taken from the advertisement, or preface, to the Grammar which accompanies the author's edition of his great quarto Dictionary. Now the several schemes which bear his own name, were doubtless all of them among those which he had that he had "*seen*;" so that he here condemns them all collectively, as he had previously condemned some of them at each reformation. Nor is the last exempted. For although he here plainly gives his vote for that common scheme which he first condemned, he does not adopt it without "some slight alterations;" and in contriving these alterations he is inconsistent with his own professions. He makes the parts of speech *eight*, thus: "1. The name or noun; 2. The

pronoun or substitute; 3. The adjective, attribute, or attributive; 4. The verb; 5. The adverb; 6. The preposition; 7. The connective or conjunction; 8. The exclamation or interjection." In his Rudiments of English Grammar, published in 1811, "to unfold the *true principles* of the language," his parts of speech were *seven*; "viz. 1. Names or nouns; 2. Substitutes or pronouns; 3. Attributes or adjectives; 4. Verbs, with their participles; 5. Modifiers or adverbs; 6. Prepositions; 7. Connectives or conjunctions." In his Philosophical and Practical Grammar, published in 1807, a book which professes to teach "the *only legitimate principles*, and established usages," of the language, a twofold division of words is adopted; first, into two general classes, primary and secondary; then into "*seven species* or parts of speech," the first two belonging to the former class, the other five to the latter; thus: "1. Names or nouns; 2. Verbs; 3. Substitutes; 4. Attributes; 5. Modifiers; 6. Prepositions; 7. Connectives." In his "Improved Grammar of the English Language," published in 1831, the same scheme is retained, but the usual names are preferred.

18. How many different schemes of classification this author invented, I know not; but he might well have saved himself the trouble of inventing any; for, so far as appears, none of his last three grammars ever came to a second edition. In the sixth edition of his "Plain and Comprehensive Grammar, grounded on the *true principles* and idioms of the language," a work which his last grammatical preface affirms to have been originally fashioned "on the model of Lowth's," the parts of speech are reckoned "*six*; nouns, articles, pronouns, adjectives, verbs, and abbreviations or particles." This work, which he says "was extensively used in the schools of this country," and continued to be in demand, he voluntarily suppressed; because, after a profitable experiment of four and twenty years, he found it so far from being grounded on "true principles," that the whole scheme then appeared to him incorrigibly bad. And, judging from this sixth edition, printed in 1800, the only one which I have seen, I cannot but concur with

him in the opinion. More than one half of the volume is a loose *Appendix* composed chiefly of notes taken from Lowth and Priestley; and there is a great want of method in what was meant for the body of the work. I imagine his several editions must have been different grammars with the same title; for such things are of no uncommon occurrence, and I cannot otherwise account for the assertion that this book was compiled "on *the model of Lowth's,* and on the same principles as [those on which] Murray has constructed his."—*Advertisement in Webster's Quarto Dict., 1st Ed.*

19. In a treatise on grammar, a bad scheme is necessarily attended with inconveniences for which no merit in the execution can possibly compensate. The first thing, therefore, which a skillful teacher will notice in a work of this kind, is the arrangement. If he find any difficulty in discovering, at sight, what it is, he will be sure it is bad; for a lucid order is what he has a right to expect from him who pretends to improve upon all the English grammarians. Dr. Webster is not the only reader of the EPEA PTEROENTA, who has been thereby prompted to meddle with the common scheme of grammar; nor is he the only one who has attempted to simplify the subject by reducing the parts of speech to *six.* John Dalton of Manchester, in 1801, in a small grammar which he dedicated to Horne Tooke, made them six, but not the same six. He would have them to be, nouns, pronouns, verbs, adverbs, conjunctions, and prepositions. This writer, like Brightland, Tooke, Fisher, and some others, insists on it that the articles are *adjectives.* Priestley, too, throwing them out of his classification, and leaving the learner to go almost through his book in ignorance of their rank, at length assigns them to the same class, in one of his notes. And so has Dr. Webster fixed them in his late valuable, but not faultless, dictionaries. But David Booth, an etymologist perhaps equally learned, in his "Introduction to an Analytical Dictionary of the English Language," declares them to be of the same species as the *pronouns;* from which he thinks it strange that they were ever separated! See *Booth's Introd.,* p. 21.

20. Now, what can be more idle, than for teachers to reject the common classification of words, and puzzle the heads of school-boys with speculations like these? It is easy to admit all that etymology can show to be true, and still justify the old arrangement of the elements of grammar. And if we depart from the common scheme, where shall we stop? Some have taught that the parts of speech are only *five*; as did the latter stoics, whose classes, according to Priscian and Harris, were these: articles, nouns appellative, nouns proper, verbs, and conjunctions. Others have made them *four*; as did Aristotle and the elder stoics, and, more recently, Milnes, Brightland, Harris, Ware, Fisher, and the author of a work on Universal Grammar, entitled Enclytica. Yet, in naming the four, each of these contrives to differ from *all the rest!* With Aristotle, they are, "nouns, verbs, articles, and conjunctions;" with Milnes, "nouns, adnouns, verbs, and particles;" with Brightland, "names, qualities, affirmations, and particles;" with Harris, "substantives, attributives, definitives, and connectives;" with Ware, "the name, the word, the assistant, the connective;" with Fisher, "names, qualities, verbs, and particles;" with the author of Enclytica, "names, verbs, modes, and connectives." But why make the classes so numerous as four? Many of the ancients, Greeks, Hebrews, and Arabians, according to Quintilian, made them *three*; and these three, according to Vossius, were nouns, verbs, and particles. "Veteres Arabes, Hebræi, et Græci, tres, non amplius, classes faciebant; l. Nomen, 2. Verbum, 3. Particula seu Dictio."—*Voss. de Anal.*, Lib. i, Cap. 1.

21. Nor is this number, *three*, quite destitute of modern supporters; though most of these come at it in an other way. D. St. Quentin, in his Rudiments of General Grammar, published in 1812, divides words into the "three general classes" last mentioned; viz., "1. Nouns, 2. Verbs, 3. Particles."—P. 5. Booth, who published the second edition of his etymological work in 1814, examining severally the ten parts of speech, and finding what he supposed to be the true origin of all the words in some of

the classes, was led to throw one into an other, till he had destroyed seven of them. Then, resolving that each word ought to be classed according to the meaning which its etymology fixes upon it, he refers the number of classes to *nature*, thus: "If, then, each [word] has a *meaning*, and is capable of raising an idea in the mind, that idea must have its prototype in nature. It must either denote an *exertion*, and is therefore a *verb*; or a *quality*, and is, in that case, an *adjective*; or it must express an *assemblage* of qualities, such as is observed to belong to some individual object, and is, on this supposition, the *name* of such object, or a *noun*. * * * We have thus given an account of the different divisions of words, and have found that the whole may be classed under the three heads of Names, Qualities, and Actions; or Nouns, Adjectives, and Verbs."—*Introd. to Analyt. Dict.*, p. 22.

22. This notion of the parts of speech, as the reader will presently see, found an advocate also in the author of the popular little story of Jack Halyard. It appears in his Philosophic Grammar published in Philadelphia in 1827. Whether the writer borrowed it from Booth, or was led into it by the light of "nature," I am unable to say: he does not appear to have derived it from the ancients. Now, if either he or the lexicographer has discovered in "nature" a prototype for this scheme of grammar, the discovery is only to be proved, and the schemes of all other grammarians, ancient or modern, must give place to it. For the reader will observe that this triad of parts is not that which is mentioned by Vossius and Quintilian. But authority may be found for reducing the number of the parts of speech yet lower. Plato, according to Harris, and the first inquirers into language, according to Horne Tooke, made them *two*; nouns and verbs, which Crombie, Dalton, M'Culloch, and some others, say, are the only parts essentially necessary for the communication of our thoughts. Those who know nothing about grammar, regard all words as of *one* class. To them, a word is simply a word; and under what other name it may come, is no concern of theirs.

23. Towards this point, tends every attempt to simplify grammar by suppressing any of the *ten* parts of speech. Nothing is gained by it; and it is a departure from the best authority. We see by what steps this kind of reasoning may descend; and we have an admirable illustration of it in the several grammatical works of William S. Cardell. I shall mention them in the order in which they appeared; and the reader may judge whether the author does not ultimately arrive at the conclusion to which the foregoing series is conducted. This writer, in his Essay on Language, reckons seven parts of speech; in his New-York Grammar, six; in his Hartford Grammar, three principal, with three others subordinate; in his Philadelphia Grammar, three only—nouns, adjectives, and verbs. Here he alleges, "The unerring plan of *nature* has established three classes of perceptions, and consequently three parts of speech."—P. 171. He says this, as if he meant to abide by it. But, on his twenty-third page, we are told, "Every adjective is either a noun or a participle." Now, by his own showing, there are no participles: he makes them all adjectives, in each of his schemes. It follows, therefore, that all his adjectives, including what others call participles, are nouns. And this reduces his three parts of speech to two, in spite of "the unerring plan of *nature!*" But even this number is more than he well believed in; for, on the twenty-first page of the book, he affirms, that, "All other terms are but derivative forms and new applications of *nouns*." So simple a thing is this method of grammar! But Neef, in his zeal for reformation, carries the anticlimax fairly off the brink; and declares, "In the grammar which shall be the work of my pupils, there shall be found no nouns, no pronouns, no articles, no participles, no verbs, no prepositions, no conjunctions, no adverbs, no interjections, no gerunds, not even one single supine. Unmercifully shall they be banished from it."—*Neef's Method of Education*, p. 60.

24. When Cardell's system appeared, several respectable men, convinced by "his powerful demonstrations," admitted that he had made "many things

in the *established doctrines* of the expounders of language appear sufficiently ridiculous;" [75] and willingly lent him the influence of their names, trusting that his admirable scheme of English grammar, in which their ignorance saw nothing but new truth, would be speedily "perfected and generally embraced." [76] Being invited by the author to a discussion of his principles, I opposed them *in his presence,* both privately and publicly; defending against him, not unsuccessfully, those doctrines which time and custom have sanctioned. And, what is remarkable, that candid opposition which Cardell himself had treated with respect, and parried in vain, was afterwards, by some of his converts, impeached of all unfairness, and even accused of wanting common sense. "No one," says Niebuhr, "ever overthrew a literary idol, without provoking the anger of its worshipers."— *Philological Museum,* Vol. i, p. 489. The certificates given in commendation of this "set of opinions," though they had no extensive effect on the public, showed full well that the signers knew little of the history of grammar; and it is the continual repetition of such things, that induces me now to dwell upon its history, for the information of those who are so liable to be deceived by exploded errors republished as novelties. A eulogist says of Cardell, "He had adopted a set of opinions, which, to most of his readers, appeared *entirely new."* A reviewer proved, that all his pretended novelties are to be found in certain grammars now forgotten, or seldom read. The former replies, Then he [Cardell,] is right—and the man is no less stupid than abusive, who finds fault; for here is proof that the former "had highly respectable authority for almost every thing he has advanced!"—See *The Friend,* Vol. ii, pp. 105 and 116, from which all the quotations in this paragraph, except one, are taken.

25. The reader may now be curious to know what these doctrines were. They were summed up by the reviewer, thus: "Our author pretends to have drawn principally from his own resources, in making up his books; and many may have supposed there is more *novelty* in them than there really is.

For instance: 1. He classes the *articles* with *adjectives*; and so did Brightland, Tooke, Fisher, Dalton, and Webster. 2. He calls the *participles, adjectives*; and so did Brightland and Tooke. 3. He make the *pronouns,* either *nouns* or *adjectives*; and so did Adam, Dalton, and others. 4. He distributes the *conjunctions* among the other parts of speech; and so did Tooke. 5. He rejects the *interjections*; and so did Valla, Sanctius, and Tooke. 6. He makes the *possessive case* an *adjective*; and so did Brightland. 7. He says our language has *no cases*; and so did Harris. 8. He calls *case, position*; and so did James Brown. 9. He reduces the adjectives to two classes, *defining* and *describing*; and so did Dalton. 10. He declares all *verbs* to be *active*; and so did Harris, (in his Hermes, Book i, Chap. ix,) though he admitted the *expediency* of the common division, and left to our author the absurdity of contending about it. Fisher also rejected the class of *neuter verbs*, and called them all *active*. 11. He reduces the *moods* to *three*, and the *tenses* to *three*; and so did Dalton, in the very same words. Fisher also made the *tenses three*, but said there *are no moods* in English. 12. He makes the *imperative mood* always *future*; and so did Harris, in 1751. Nor did the doctrine originate with him; for Brightland, a hundred years ago, [about 1706,] ascribed it to some of his predecessors. 13. He reduces the whole of our *syntax* to about *thirty lines*; and two thirds of these are useless; for Dr. Johnson expressed it quite as fully in *ten*. But their explanations are both good for nothing; and Wallis, more wisely, omitted it altogether."— *The Friend*, Vol. ii, p. 59.

26. Dr. Webster says, in a marginal note to the preface of his Philosophical Grammar, "Since the days of *Wallis*, who published a Grammar of the English Language, in Latin, in the reign of Charles II.[,] from which Johnson and Lowth borrowed most of their rules, *little improvement* has been made in English grammar. Lowth supplied some valuable criticisms, most of which however respect obsolete phrases; but many of his criticisms are extremely erroneous, and they have had an ill

effect, in perverting the true idioms of our language. Priestley furnished a number of new and useful observations on the peculiar phrases of the English language. To which may be added some good remarks of Blair and Campbell, interspersed with many errors. Murray, not having mounted to the original sources of information, and professing only to select and arrange the rules and criticisms of preceding writers, has furnished little or nothing new. Of the numerous compilations of inferior character, it may be affirmed, that they have added nothing to the stock of grammatical knowledge." And the concluding sentence of this work, as well as of his Improved Grammar, published in 1831, extends the censure as follows: "It is not the English language only whose history and principles are yet to be illustrated; but the grammars and dictionaries of *all other* languages, with which I have any acquaintance, must be revised and corrected, before their elements and true construction can be fully understood." In an advertisement to the grammar prefixed to his quarto American Dictionary, the Doctor is yet more severe upon books of this sort. "I close," says he, "with the single remark, that from all the observations I have been able to make, I am convinced the dictionaries and grammars which have been used in our seminaries of learning for the last forty or fifty years, are *so incorrect and imperfect* that they have introduced or sanctioned more errors than they have amended; in other words, had the people of England and of these States been left to learn the pronunciation and construction of their vernacular language solely by tradition, and the reading of good authors, the language would have been spoken and written with more purity than it has been and now is, by those who have learned to adjust their language by the rules which dictionaries prescribe."

27. Little and much are but relative terms; yet when we look back to the period in which English grammar was taught only in Latin, it seems extravagant to say, that "little improvement has been made" in it since. I have elsewhere expressed a more qualified sentiment. "That the grammar of

our language has made considerable progress since the days of Swift, who wrote a petty treatise on the subject, is sufficiently evident; but whoever considers what remains to be done, cannot but perceive how ridiculous are many of the boasts and felicitations which we have heard on that topic." [77] Some further notice will now be taken of that progress, and of the writers who have been commonly considered the chief promoters of it, but especially of such as have not been previously mentioned in a like connexion. Among these may be noticed *William Walker*, the preceptor of Sir Isaac Newton, a teacher and grammarian of extraordinary learning, who died in 1684. He has left us sundry monuments of his taste and critical skill: one is his "Treatise of English Particles,"—a work of great labour and merit, but useless to most people now-a-days, because it explains the English in Latin; an other, his "Art of Teaching Improv'd,"—which is also an able treatise, and apparently well adapted to its object, "the Grounding of a Young Scholar in the Latin Tongue." In the latter, are mentioned other works of his, on "*Rhetorick*, and *Logick*" which I have not seen.

28. In 1706, *Richard Johnson* published an octavo volume of more than four hundred pages, entitled, "Grammatical Commentaries; being an Apparatus to a New National Grammar: by way of animadversion upon the falsities, obscurities, redundancies and defects of Lily's System now in use." This is a work of great acuteness, labour, and learning; and might be of signal use to any one who should undertake to prepare a new or improved Latin grammar: of which, in my opinion, we have yet urgent need. The English grammarian may also peruse it with advantage, if he has a good knowledge of Latin—and without such knowledge he must be ill prepared for his task. This work is spoken of and quoted by some of the early English grammarians; but the hopes of the writer do not appear to have been realized. His book was not calculated to supply the place of the common one; for the author thought it impracticable to make a new grammar, suitable for boys, and at the same time to embrace in it proofs sufficient to remove the prejudices of teachers in favour of the old. King Henry's edict in support of Lily, was yet in force, backed by all the partiality which long habit creates; and Johnson's learning, and labour, and zeal, were admired, and praised, and soon forgot.

29. Near the beginning of the last century, some of the generous wits of the reign of Queen Anne, seeing the need there was of greater attention to their vernacular language, and of a grammar more properly English than any then in use, produced a book with which the later writers on the same subjects, would have done well to have made themselves better acquainted. It is entitled "A Grammar of the English Tongue; with the Arts of Logick, Rhetorick, Poetry, &c. Illustrated with useful Notes; giving the Grounds and Reasons of Grammar in General. The Whole making a Compleat System of an English Education. *Published by* JOHN BRIGHTLAND, for the Use of the Schools of Great Britain and Ireland." It is ingeniously recommended in a certificate by Sir Richard Steele, or the Tattler, under the fictitious name

of Isaac Bickerstaff, Esq., and in a poem of forty-three lines, by Nahum Tate, poet laureate to her Majesty. It is a duodecimo volume of three hundred pages; a work of no inconsiderable merit and originality; and written in a style which, though not faultless, has scarcely been surpassed by any English grammarian since. I quote it as Brightland's:[78] who were the real authors, does not appear. It seems to be the work of more than one, and perhaps the writers of the Tattler were the men. My copy is of the seventh edition, London, printed for Henry Lintot, 1746. It is evidently the work of very skillful hands; yet is it not in all respects well planned or well executed. It unwisely reduces the parts of speech to four; gives them new names; and rejects more of the old system than the schools could be made willing to give up. Hence it does not appear to have been very extensively adopted.

30. It is now about a hundred and thirty years, since *Dr. Swift*, in a public remonstrance addressed to the Earl of Oxford, complained of the imperfect state of our language, and alleged in particular, that "in many instances it offended against every part of grammar." [79] Fifty years afterward, *Dr. Lowth* seconded this complaint, and pressed it home upon the polite and the learned. "Does he mean," says the latter, "that the English language, as it is spoken by the politest part of the nation, and as it stands in the writings of the most approved authors, often offends against every part of grammar? *Thus far, I am afraid the charge is true.*"—*Lowth's Grammar, Preface*, p. iv. Yet the learned Doctor, to whom much praise has been justly ascribed for the encouragement which he gave to this neglected study, attempted nothing more than "A Short Introduction to English Grammar;" which, he says, "was calculated for the learner *even of the lowest class*:" and those who would enter more deeply into the subject, he referred to *Harris*; whose work is not an English grammar, but "A Philosophical Inquiry concerning Universal Grammar." Lowth's Grammar was first published in 1758. At the commencement of his preface, the reverend author, after acknowledging the

enlargement, polish, and refinement, which the language had received during the preceding two hundred years, ventures to add, "but, whatever other improvements it may have received, it hath made *no advances* in grammatical accuracy." I do not quote this assertion to affirm it literally true, in all its apparent breadth; but there is less reason to boast of the correctness even now attained, than to believe that the writers on grammar are not the authors who have in general come nearest to it in practice. Nor have the ablest authors always produced the best compends for the literary instruction of youth.

31. The treatises of the learned doctors Harris, Lowth, Johnson, Ash, Priestley, Horne Tooke, Crombie, Coote, and Webster, owe their celebrity not so much to their intrinsic fitness for school instruction, as to the literary reputation of the writers. Of *Harris's Hermes,* (which, in comparison with our common grammars, is indeed a work of much ingenuity and learning, full of interesting speculations, and written with great elegance both of style and method,) *Dr. Lowth* says, it is "the most beautiful and perfect example of analysis, that has been exhibited since the days of Aristotle."—*Preface to Gram.,* p. x. But these two authors, if their works be taken together, as the latter intended they should be, supply no sufficient course of English grammar. The instructions of the one are too limited, and those of the other are not specially directed to the subject.

32. *Dr. Johnson,* who was practically one of the greatest grammarians that ever lived, and who was very nearly coetaneous with both Harris and Lowth, speaks of the state of English grammar in the following terms: "I found our speech copious without order, and energetick *without rules*: wherever I turned my view, there was perplexity to be disentangled, and confusion to be regulated."—*Preface to Dict.,* p. 1. Again: "Having therefore *no assistance but from general grammar*, I applied myself to the perusal of our writers; and noting whatever might be of use to ascertain or

illustrate any word or phrase, accumulated in time the materials of a dictionary."—*Ibid.* But it is not given to any one man to do every thing; else, Johnson had done it. His object was, to compile a dictionary, rather than to compose a grammar, of our language. To lexicography, grammar is necessary, as a preparation; but, as a purpose, it is merely incidental. Dr. Priestley speaks of Johnson thus: "I must not conclude this preface, without making my acknowledgements to Mr. *Johnson,* whose admirable dictionary has been of the greatest use to me in the study of our language. It is pity he had not formed as just, and as extensive an idea of English grammar. Perhaps this very useful work may still be reserved for his distinguished abilities in this way."—*Priestley's Grammar, Preface,* p. xxiii. Dr. Johnson's English Grammar is all comprised in fourteen pages, and of course it is very deficient. The syntax he seems inclined entirely to omit, as (he says) Wallis did, and Ben Jonson had better done; but, for form's sake, he condescends to bestow upon it ten short lines.

33. My point here is, that the best grammarians have left much to be done by him who may choose to labour for the further improvement of English grammar; and that a man may well deserve comparative praise, who has not reached perfection in a science like this. Johnson himself committed many errors, some of which I shall hereafter expose; yet I cannot conceive that the following judgement of his works was penned without some bias of prejudice: "Johnson's merit ought not to be denied to him; but his dictionary is the most imperfect and faulty, and the least valuable *of any*[80] of his productions; and that share of merit which it possesses, makes it by so much the more hurtful. I rejoice, however, that though the least valuable, he found it the most profitable: for I could never read his preface without shedding a tear. And yet it must be confessed, that his *grammar* and *history* and *dictionary* of what *he calls* the English language, are in all respects (except the bulk of the *latter*[81]) most truly contemptible performances; and a reproach to the learning and industry of a nation which could receive

them with the slightest approbation. Nearly one third of this dictionary is as much the language of the Hottentots as of the English; and it would be no difficult matter so to translate any one of the plainest and most popular numbers of the *Spectator* into the language of this dictionary, that no mere Englishman, though well read in his own language, would he able to comprehend one sentence of it. It appears to be a work of labour, and yet is in truth one of the most idle performances ever offered to the public; compiled by an author who possessed not one single requisite for the undertaking, and (being a publication of a set of booksellers) owing its success to that very circumstance which alone must make it impossible that it should deserve success."—*Tooke's Diversions of Purley*, Vol. i, p. 182.

34. *Dr. Ash's* "Grammatical Institutes, or Easy Introduction to Dr. Lowth's English Grammar," is a meagre performance, the ease of which consists in nothing but its brevity. *Dr. Priestley*, who in the preface to his third edition acknowledges his obligations to Johnson, and also to Lowth, thought it premature to attempt an English grammar; and contented himself with publishing a few brief "Rudiments," with a loose appendix consisting of "Notes and Observations, for the use of those who have made some proficiency in the language." He says, "With respect to our own language, there seems to be a kind of claim upon all who make use of it, to do something for its improvement; and the best thing we can do for this purpose at present, is, to exhibit its actual structure, and the varieties with which it is used. When these are once distinctly pointed out, and generally attended to, the best forms of speech, and those which are most agreeable to the analogy of the language, will soon recommend themselves, and come into general use; and when, by this means, the language shall be written with sufficient uniformity, we may hope to see a complete grammar of it. At present, *it is by no means ripe for such a work*;[82] but we may approximate to it very fast, if all persons who are qualified to make remarks upon it, will give a little attention to the subject. In such a case, a few years

might be sufficient to complete it."—*Priestley's Grammar, Preface*, p. xv. In point of time, both Ash and Priestley expressly claim priority to Lowth, for their first editions; but the former having allowed his work to be afterwards entitled an Introduction to Lowth's, and the latter having acknowledged some improvements in his from the same source, they have both been regarded as later authors.

35. The great work of the learned etymologist *John Horne Tooke*, consists of two octavo volumes, entitled, "EPEA PTEROENTA, or the Diversions of Purley." This work explains, with admirable sagacity, the origin and primitive import of many of the most common yet most obscure English words; and is, for that reason, a valuable performance. But as it contains nothing respecting the construction of the language, and embraces no proper system of grammatical doctrines, it is a great error to suppose that the common principles of practical grammar ought to give place to such instructions, or even be modelled according to what the author proves to be true in respect to the origin of particular words. The common grammarians were less confuted by him, than many of his readers have imagined; and it ought not to be forgotten that his purpose was as different from theirs, as are their schemes of Grammar from the plan of his critical "Diversions." In this connexion may be mentioned an other work of similar size and purpose, but more comprehensive in design; the "History of European Languages," by that astonishing linguist the late *Dr. Alexander Murray*. This work was left unfinished by its lamented author; but it will remain a monument of erudition never surpassed, acquired in spite of wants and difficulties as great as diligence ever surmounted. Like Tooke's volumes, it is however of little use to the mere English scholar. It can be read to advantage only by those who are acquainted with several other languages. The works of *Crombie* and *Coote* are more properly essays or dissertations, than elementary systems of grammar.

36. The number of English grammars has now become so very great, that not even a general idea of the comparative merits or defects of each can here be given. I have examined with some diligence all that I have had opportunity to obtain; but have heard of several which I have never yet seen. Whoever is curious to examine at large what has been published on this subject, and thus to qualify himself to judge the better of any new grammar, may easily make a collection of one or two hundred bearing different names. There are also many works not called grammars, from which our copyists have taken large portions of their compilations. Thus Murray confessedly copied from ten authors; five of whom are Beattie, Sheridan, Walker, Blair, and Campbell. Dr. Beattie, who acquired great celebrity as a teacher, poet, philosopher, and logician, was well skilled in grammar; but he treated the subject only in critical disquisitions, and not in any distinct elementary work adapted to general use. Sheridan and Walker, being lexicographers, confined themselves chiefly to orthography and pronunciation. Murray derived sundry principles from the writings of each; but the English Grammar prepared by the latter, was written, I think, several years later than Murray's. The learned doctors Blair and Campbell wrote on rhetoric, and not on the elementary parts of grammar. Of the two, the latter is by far the more accurate writer. Blair is fluent and easy, but he furnishes not a little false syntax; Campbell's Philosophy of Rhetoric is a very valuable treatise. To these, and five or six other authors whom I have noticed, was Lindley Murray "principally indebted for his materials." Thus far of the famous contributors to English grammar. The Lectures on Rhetoric and Oratory, delivered at Harvard University by John Quincy Adams, and published in two octavo volumes in 1810, are such as do credit even to that great man; but they descend less to verbal criticism, and enter less into the peculiar province of the grammarian, than do most other works of a similar title.

37. Some of the most respectable authors or compilers of more general systems of English grammar for the use of schools, are the writer of the British Grammar, Bicknell, Buchanan, William Ward, Alexander Murray the schoolmaster, Mennye, Fisher, Lindley Murray, Penning, W. Allen, Grant, David Blair, Lennie, Guy, Churchill. To attempt any thing like a review or comparative estimate of these, would protract this introduction beyond all reasonable bounds; and still others would be excluded, which are perhaps better entitled to notice. Of mere modifiers and abridgers, the number is so great, and the merit or fame so little, that I will not trespass upon the reader's patience by any further mention of them or their works. Whoever takes an accurate and comprehensive view of the history and present state of this branch of learning, though he may not conclude, with Dr. Priestley, that it is premature to attempt a complete grammar of the language, can scarcely forbear to coincide with Dr. Barrow, in the opinion that among all the treatises heretofore produced no such grammar is found. "Some superfluities have been expunged, some mistakes have been rectified, and some obscurities have been cleared; still, however, that all the grammars used in our different schools, public as well as private, are disgraced by errors or defects, is a complaint as just as it is frequent and loud."—*Barrow's Essays*, p. 83.

38. Whether, in what I have been enabled to do, there will be found a remedy for this complaint, must be referred to the decision of others. Upon the probability of effecting this, I have been willing to stake some labour; how much, and with what merit, let the candid and discerning, when they shall have examined for themselves, judge. It is certain that we have hitherto had, of our language, no complete grammar. The need of such a work I suppose to be at this time in no small degree felt, especially by those who conduct our higher institutions of learning; and my ambition has been to produce one which might deservedly stand along side of the Port-Royal Latin and Greek Grammars, or of the Grammaire des Grammaires of

Girault Du Vivier. If this work is unworthy to aspire to such rank, let the patrons of English literature remember that the achievement of my design is still a desideratum. We surely have no other book which might, in any sense, have been called "*the Grammar of English Grammars;*" none, which, either by excellence, or on account of the particular direction of its criticism, might take such a name. I have turned the eyes of Grammar, in an especial manner, upon the conduct of her own household; and if, from this volume, the reader acquire a more just idea of *the grammar* which is displayed in *English grammars,* he will discover at least one reason for the title which has been bestowed upon the work. Such as the book is, I present it to the public, without pride, without self-seeking, and without anxiety: knowing that most of my readers will be interested in estimating it *justly*; that no true service, freely rendered to learning, can fail of its end; and that no achievement merits aught with Him who graciously supplies all ability. The opinions expressed in it have been formed with candour, and are offered with submission. If in any thing they are erroneous, there are those who can detect their faults. In the language of an ancient master, the earnest and assiduous *Despauter*, I invite the correction of the candid: "Nos quoque, quantumcunque diligentes, cùm a candidis tùm a lividis carpemur: a candidis interdum justè; quos oro, ut de erratis omnibus amicè me admoneant—erro nonnunquam quia homo sum."

Grammar, as an art, is the power of reading, writing, and speaking correctly. As an acquisition, it is the essential skill of scholarship. As a study, it is the practical science which teaches the right use of language.

An English Grammar is a book which professes to explain the nature and structure of the English language; and to show, on just authority, what is, and what is not, good English.

ENGLISH GRAMMAR, in itself, is the art of reading, writing, and speaking the English language correctly. It implies, in the adept, such knowledge as enables him to avoid improprieties of speech; to correct any errors that may occur in literary compositions; and to parse, or explain grammatically, whatsoever is rightly written.

To read is to perceive what is written or printed, so as to understand the words, and be able to utter them with their proper sounds.

To write is to express words and thoughts by letters, or characters, made with a pen or other instrument.

To speak is to utter words orally, in order that they may be heard and understood.

Grammar, like every other liberal art, can be properly taught only by a regular analysis, or systematic elucidation, of its component parts or principles; and these parts or principles must be made known chiefly by means of definitions and examples, rules and exercises.

A *perfect definition* of any thing or class of things is such a description of it, as distinguishes that entire thing or class from every thing else, by briefly telling *what it is*.

An *example* is a particular instance or model, serving to prove or illustrate some given proposition or truth.

A *rule of grammar* is some law, more or less general, by which custom regulates and prescribes the right use of language.

An *exercise* is some technical performance required of the learner in order to bring his knowledge and skill into practice.

LANGUAGE, in the primitive sense of the term, embraced only vocal expression, or human speech uttered by the mouth; but after letters were invented to represent articulate sounds, language became twofold, *spoken* and *written*, so that the term, *language*, now signifies, *any series of sounds or letters formed into words and employed for the expression of thought*.

Of the composition of language we have also two kinds, *prose* and *verse*; the latter requiring a certain number and variety of syllables in each line, but the former being free from any such restraint.

The *least parts* of written language are letters; of spoken language, syllables; of language significant in each part, words; of language combining thought, phrases; of language subjoining sense, clauses; of language coördinating sense, members; of language completing sense, sentences.

A discourse, or narration, of any length, is but a series of sentences; which, when written, must be separated by the proper points, that the meaning and relation of all the words may be quickly and clearly perceived by the reader, and the whole be uttered as the sense requires.

In extended compositions, a sentence is usually less than a paragraph; a paragraph, less than a section; a section, less than a chapter; a chapter, less than a book; a book, less than a volume; and a volume, less than the entire work.

The common order of *literary division*, then, is; of a large work, into volumes; of volumes, into books; of books, into chapters; of chapters, into sections; of sections, into paragraphs; of paragraphs, into sentences; of sentences, into members; of members, into clauses; of clauses, into phrases; of phrases, into words; of words, into syllables; of syllables, into letters.

But it rarely happens that any one work requires the use of all these divisions; and we often assume some natural distinction and order of parts, naming each as we find it; and also subdivide into articles, verses, cantoes, stanzas, and other portions, as the nature of the subject suggests.

Grammar is divided into four parts; namely, Orthography, Etymology, Syntax, and Prosody.

Orthography treats of letters, syllables, separate words, and spelling.

Etymology treats of the different *parts of speech*, with their classes and modifications.

Syntax treats of the relation, agreement, government, and arrangement of words in sentences.

Prosody treats of punctuation, utterance, figures, and versification.

OBSERVATIONS.

OBS. 1.—In the Introduction to this work, have been taken many views of the study, or general science, of grammar; many notices of its history, with sundry criticisms upon its writers or critics; and thus language has often been presented to the reader's consideration, either as a whole, or with broader scope than belongs to the teaching of its particular forms. We come now to the work of *analyzing* our own tongue, and of laying down those special rules and principles which should guide us in the use of it, whether in speech or in writing. The author intends to dissent from other grammarians no more than they are found to dissent from truth and reason; nor will he expose their errors further than is necessary for the credit of the science and the information of the learner. A candid critic can have no satisfaction merely in finding fault with other men's performances. But the facts are not to be concealed, that many pretenders to grammar have shown themselves exceedingly superficial in their knowledge, as well as slovenly in their practice; and that many vain composers of books have proved themselves *despisers* of this study, by the abundance of their inaccuracies, and the obviousness of their solecisms.

OBS. 2.—Some grammarians have taught that the word *language* is of much broader signification, than that which is given to it in the definition above. I confine it to speech and writing. For the propriety of this limitation, and against those authors who describe the thing otherwise, I appeal to the common sense of mankind. One late writer defines it thus: "LANGUAGE is *any means* by which one *person* communicates his *ideas* to *another*."—*Sanders's Spelling-Book*, p. 7. The following is the explanation of an other slack thinker: "One may, by speaking or by writing, (and sometimes *by motions*,) communicate his thoughts to others. *The process* by which this is done, is called LANGUAGE.—*Language* is *the expression* of thought *and feeling*."—*S. W. Clark's Practical Gram.*, p. 7. Dr. Webster goes much further, and says, "LANGUAGE, in its most extensive sense, is the instrument or means of communicating ideas *and affections* of the mind *and body*, from one *animal to another*. In this sense, *brutes possess the power of language*; for by various inarticulate sounds, they make known their wants, desires, and sufferings."— *Philosophical Gram.*, p. 11; *Improved Gram.*, p. 5. This latter definition the author of that vain book, "*the District School*," has adopted in his chapter on Grammar. Sheridan, the celebrated actor and orthoëpist, though he seems to confine language to the human species, gives it such an extension as to make words no necessary part of its essence. "The first thought," says he, "that would occur to every one, who had not properly considered the point, is, that language is composed of words. And yet, this is so far from being an adequate idea of language, that the point in which most men think its very essence to consist, is not even a necessary property of language. For language, in its full extent, means, any way or method whatsoever, by which *all that passes in the mind of one man*, may be manifested to another."—*Sheridan's Lectures on Elocution*, p. 129. Again: "I have already *shown*, that words are, in their own nature, *no essential part of language*, and are only considered so through custom."—*Ib.* p. 135.

OBS. 3.—According to S. Kirkham's notion, "LANGUAGE, in its most extensive sense, implies those signs by which *men and brutes*, communicate *to each other* their thoughts, affections and desires."—*Kirkham's English Gram.*, p. 16. Again: "*The language of brutes* consists in the use of those inarticulate sounds by which they express *their thoughts and affections*."—*Ib.* To me it seems a shameful abuse of speech, and a vile descent from the dignity of grammar, to make the voices of "*brutes*" any part of language, as taken in a literal sense. We might with far more propriety raise our conceptions of it to the spheres above, and construe literally the metaphors of David, who ascribes to the starry heavens, both "*speech*" and "*language,*" "*voice*" and "*words,*" daily "*uttered*" and everywhere "*heard.*" See *Psalm* xix.

OBS. 4.—But, strange as it may seem, Kirkham, commencing his instructions with the foregoing definition of language, proceeds to divide it, agreeably to this notion, into two sorts, *natural* and *artificial*; and affirms that the former "is common both to man and brute," and that the language which is peculiar to man, the language which consists of *words*, is altogether an *artificial invention*:[83] thereby contradicting at once a host of the most celebrated grammarians and philosophers, and that without appearing to know it. But this is the less strange, since he immediately forgets his own definition and division of the subject, and as plainly contradicts himself. Without limiting the term at all, without excluding his fanciful "*language of brutes,*" he says, on the next leaf, "*Language* is *conventional*, and not only *invented*, but, in its progressive advancement, *varied for purposes of practical convenience.* Hence it assumes *any and every form* which those who make use of it, choose to give it."—*Kirkham's Gram.*, p. 18. This, though scarcely more rational than his "*natural language of men and brutes,*" plainly annihilates that questionable section of grammatical science, whether brutal or human, by making all language a thing "*conventional*" and "*invented.*" In short, it leaves no ground at all for any grammatical science of a positive character, because it resolves all forms of language into the irresponsible will of those who utter any words, sounds, or noises.

OBS. 5.—Nor is this gentleman more fortunate in his explanation of what may really be called language. On one page, he says, "*Spoken language* or *speech*, is made up of articulate sounds uttered by the human voice."—*Kirkham's Gram.*, p. 17. On the next, "The most important use of *that faculty called speech*, is, to convey our thoughts to others."—*Ib.*, p. 18. Thus the grammarian who, in the same short paragraph, seems to "defy the ingenuity of man to give his words any other meaning than that which he himself intends *them to express*," (*Ib.*, p. 19,) either writes so badly as to make any ordinary false syntax appear trivial, or actually conceives man to be the inventor of one of his own *faculties*. Nay, docs he not make man the contriver of that "natural language" which he possesses "in common with the brutes?" a language "*The meaning of which*," he says, "*all the different animals perfectly understand*?"—See his *Gram.*, p. 16. And if this notion again be true, does it not follow, that a horse knows perfectly well what horned cattle mean by their bellowing, or a flock of geese by their gabbling? I should not have noticed these things, had not the book which teaches them, been made popular by *a thousand* imposing attestations to its excellence and accuracy. For grammar has nothing at all to do with inarticulate voices, or the imaginary languages of *brutes*. It is scope enough for one science to explain all the languages, dialects, and speeches, that lay claim to *reason*. We need not enlarge the field, by descending

"To beasts, whom[84] God on their creation-day
Created mute to all articulate sound."—*Milton.*[85]

ORTHOGRAPHY.

ORTHOGRAPHY treats of letters, syllables, separate words, and spelling.

CHAPTER I.—OF LETTERS.

A *Letter* is an alphabetic character, which commonly represents some elementary sound of the human voice, some element of speech.

An elementary sound of the human voice, or an element of speech, is one of the simple sounds which compose a spoken language. The sound of a letter is commonly called its *power*: when any letter of a word is not sounded, it is said to be *silent* or *mute*. The letters in the English alphabet, are twenty-six; the simple or primary sounds which they represent, are about thirty-six or thirty-seven.

A knowledge of the letters consists in an acquaintance with these *four sorts of things*; their *names*, their *classes*, their *powers*, and their *forms*.

The letters are written, or printed, or painted, or engraved, or embossed, in an infinite variety of shapes and sizes; and yet are always *the same*, because their essential properties do not change, and their names, classes, and powers, are mostly permanent.

The following are some of the different sorts of types, or styles of letters, with which every reader should be early acquainted:—

1. The Roman: A a, B b, C c, D d, E e, F f, G g, H h, I i, J j, K k, L l, M m, N n, o, P p, Q q, R r, S s, T t, U u, V v, W w, X x, Y y, Z z.

2. The Italic: *A a, B b, C c, D d, E e, F f, G g, H h, I i, J j, K k, L l, M m, N n, o, P p, Q q, R r, S s, T t, U u, V v, W w, X x, Y y, Z z.*

3. The Script: [Script: A a, B b, C c, D d, E e, F f, G g, H h, I i, J j, K k, L l, M m, N n, o, P p, Q q, R r, S s, T t, U u, V v, W w, X x, Y y, Z z.]

4. The Old English: [Old English: A a, B b, C c, D d, E e, F f, G g, H h, I i, J j, K k, L l, M m, N n, o, P p, Q q, R r, S s, T t, U u, V v, W w, X x, Y y, Z z.]

OBSERVATIONS.

OBS. 1.—A letter *consists* not in the figure only, or in the power only, but in the figure and power united; as an ambassador consists not in the man only, or in the commission only, but in the man commissioned. The figure and the power, therefore, are necessary to constitute the letter; and a name is as necessary, to call it by, teach it, or tell what it is. The *class* of a letter is determined by the nature of its power, or sound; as the ambassador is plenipotentiary or otherwise, according to the extent of his commission. To all but the deaf and dumb, written language is the representative of that which is spoken; so that, in the view of people in general, the powers of the letters are habitually identified with their sounds, and are conceived to be nothing else. Hence any given sound, or modification of sound, which all men can produce at pleasure, when arbitrarily associated with a written sign, or conventional character, constitutes what is called *a letter*. Thus we may produce the sounds of *a, e, o*, then, by a particular compression of the organs of utterance, modify them all, into *ba, be, bo*, or *fa, fe, fo*; and we shall see that *a, e*, and *o*, are letters of one sort, and *b* and *f* of an other. By *elementary* or *articulate* sounds,[86] then, we mean not only the simple tones of the voice itself, but the modifying stops and turns which are given them in speech, and marked by letters: the real voices constituting vowels; and their modifications, consonants.

OBS. 2.—A mere mark to which no sound or power is ever given, cannot be a letter; though it may, like the marks used for punctuation, deserve a name and a place in grammar. Commas, semicolons, and the like, represent *silence,* rather than sounds, and are therefore not letters. Nor are the Arabic figures, which represent entire *words,* nor again any symbols standing for *things,* (as the astronomic marks for the sun, the moon, the planets,) to be confounded with letters; because the representative of any word or number, of any name or thing, differs widely in its power, from the sign of a simple elementary sound: i. e., from any constituent *part* of a written word. The first letter of a word or name does indeed sometimes stand for the whole, and is still a letter; but it is so, as being the first element of the word, and not as being the representative of the whole.

OBS. 3.—In their definitions of vowels and consonants, many grammarians have resolved letters into *sounds only*; as, "A Vowel is an articulate *sound,*" &c.—"A Consonant is an articulate *sound,*" &c.—*L. Murray's Gram.,* p. 7. But this confounding of the visible signs with the things which they signify, is very far from being a true account of either. Besides, letters combined are capable of a certain mysterious power which is independent of all sound, though speech, doubtless, is what they properly represent. In practice, almost all the letters may occasionally happen to be *silent*; yet are they not, in these cases, necessarily useless. The deaf and dumb also, to whom none of the letters express or represent sounds, may be taught to read and write understandingly. They even learn in some way to distinguish the accented from the unaccented syllables, and to have some notion of *quantity*, or of something else equivalent to it; for some of them, it is said, can compose verses according to the rules of prosody. Hence it would appear, that the powers of the letters are not, of necessity, identified with their sounds; the things being in some respect distinguishable, though the terms are commonly taken as synonymous. The fact is, that a word, whether spoken or written, is of itself *significant*, whether its corresponding form be known or not. Hence, in the one form, it may be perfectly intelligible to the illiterate, and in the other, to the educated deaf and dumb; while, to the learned who hear and speak, either form immediately suggests the other, with the meaning common to both.

OBS. 4.—Our knowledge of letters rises no higher than to the forms used by the ancient Hebrews and Phoenicians. Moses is supposed to have written in characters which were nearly the same as those called Samaritan, but his writings have come to us in an alphabet more beautiful and regular, called the Chaldee or Chaldaic, which is said to have been made by Ezra the scribe, when he wrote out a new copy of the law, after the rebuilding of the temple. Cadmus carried the Phoenician alphabet into Greece, where it was subsequently altered and enlarged. The small letters were not invented till about the seventh century of our era. The Latins, or Romans, derived most of their capitals from the Greeks; but their small letters, if they had any, were made afterwards among themselves. This alphabet underwent various changes, and received very great improvements, before it became that beautiful series of characters which we now use, under the name of *Roman letters*. Indeed these particular forms, which are now justly preferred by many nations, are said to have been adopted after the invention of printing. "The Roman letters were first used by Sweynheim and Pannartz, printers who settled at Rome, in 1467. The earliest work printed wholly in this character in England, is said to have been Lily's or Paul's Accidence, printed by Richard Pinson, 1518. The Italic letters were invented by Aldus Manutius at Rome, towards the close of the fifteenth century, and were first used in an edition of Virgil, in 1501."—*Constables Miscellany*, Vol. xx, p. 147. The Saxon alphabet was mostly Roman. Not more than one quarter of the letters have other forms. But the changes, though few, give to a printed page a very different appearance. Under William the Conqueror, this alphabet was superseded by the modern Gothic, Old English, or Black letter; which, in its turn, happily gave place to the present Roman. The Germans still use a type similar to the Old English, but not so heavy.

OBS. 5.—I have suggested that a true knowledge of the letters implies an acquaintance with their *names*, their *classes*, their *powers*, and their *forms*. Under these four heads, therefore, I shall briefly present what seems most worthy of the learner's attention at first, and shall reserve for the appendix a more particular account of these important elements. The most common and the most useful things are not those about which we are in general most inquisitive. Hence many, who think themselves sufficiently acquainted with the letters, do in fact know but very little about them. If a person is able to read some easy book, he is apt to suppose he has no more to learn respecting the letters; or he neglects the minute study of these elements, because he sees what words they make, and can amuse himself with stories of things more interesting. But merely to understand common English, is a very small qualification for him who aspires to scholarship, and especially for a *teacher*. For one may do this, and even be a great reader, without ever being able to name the letters properly, or to pronounce such syllables as *ca, ce, ci, co, cu, cy*, without getting half of them wrong. No one can ever teach an art more perfectly than he has learned it; and if we neglect the *elements* of grammar, our attainments must needs be proportionately unsettled and superficial.

I. NAMES OF THE LETTERS. The *names* of the letters, as now commonly spoken
and written in English, are *A, Bee, Cee, Dee, E, Eff, Gee, Aitch, I, Jay, Kay, Ell, Em, En, O, Pee, Kue, Ar, Ess, Tee, U, Vee, Double-u, Ex, Wy, Zee.*

OBSERVATIONS.

OBS. 1.—With the learning and application of these names, our literary education begins; with a continual rehearsal of them in spelling, it is for a long time carried on; nor can we ever dispense with them, but by substituting others, or by ceasing to mention the things thus named. What is obviously indispensable, needs no proof of its importance. But I know not whether it has ever been noticed, that these names, like those of the days of the week, are worthy of particular distinction, for their own nature. They are words of a very peculiar kind, being nouns that are at once *both proper and common*. For, in respect to rank, character, and design, each letter is a thing strictly individual and identical—that is, it is ever one and the same; yet, in an other respect, it is a comprehensive sort, embracing individuals both various and numberless. Thus every B is a *b*, make it as you will; and can be nothing else than that same letter b, though you make it in a thousand different fashions, and multiply it after each pattern innumerably. Here, then, we see individuality combined at once with great diversity, and infinite multiplicity; and it is *to this combination*, that letters owe their wonderful power of transmitting thought. Their *names*, therefore, should always be written with capitals, as proper nouns, at least in the singular number; and should form the plural regularly, as ordinary appellatives. Thus: (if we adopt the names now most generally used in English schools:) *A, Aes; Bee, Bees; Cee, Cees; Dee, Dees; E, Ees; Eff, Effs; Gee, Gees; Aitch, Aitches; I, Ies; Jay, Jays; Kay, Kays; Ell, Ells; Em, Ems; En, Ens; O,*

Oes; Pee, Pees; Kue, Kues; Ar, Ars; Ess, Esses; Tee, Tees; U, Ues; Vee, Vees; Double-u, Double-ues; Ex, Exes; Wy, Wies; Zee, Zees.

OBS. 2.—The names of the letters, as expressed in the modern languages, are mostly framed *with reference* to their powers, or sounds. Yet is there in English no letter of which the name is always identical with its power: for *A, E, I, O,* and *U,* are the only letters which can name themselves, and all these have other sounds than those which their names express. The simple powers of the other letters are so manifestly insufficient to form any name, and so palpable is the difference between the nature and the name of each, that did we not know how education has been trifled with, it would be hard to believe even Murray, when he says, "They are frequently confounded by writers on grammar. Observations and reasonings on the *name,* are often applied to explain the *nature* of a consonant; and by this means the student is led into error and perplexity."—*L. Murray's Gram.,* 8vo, p. 8. The confounding of names with the things for which they stand, implies, unquestionably, great carelessness in the use of speech, and great indistinctness of apprehension in respect to things; yet so common is this error, that Murray himself has many times fallen into it.[87] Let the learner therefore be on his guard, remembering that grammar, both in its study and in its practice, requires the constant exercise of a rational discernment. Those letters which name themselves, take for their names those sounds which they usually represent at the end of an accented syllable; thus the names, *A, E, I, O, U,* are uttered with the sounds given to the same letters in the first syllables of the other names, *Abel, Enoch, Isaac, Obed, Urim*; or in the first syllables of the common words, *paper, penal, pilot, potent, pupil.* The other letters, most of which can never be perfectly sounded alone, have names in which their powers are combined with other sounds more vocal; as, *Bee, Cee, Dee,—Ell, Em, En,—Jay, Kay, Kue.* But in this respect the terms *Aitch* and *Double-u* are irregular; because they have no obvious reference to the powers of the letters thus named.

OBS. 3.—Letters, like all other things, must be learned and spoken of *by their names*; nor can they be spoken of otherwise; yet, as the simple characters are better known and more easily exhibited than their written names, the former are often substituted for the latter, and are read as the words for which they are assumed. Hence the orthography of these words has hitherto been left too much to mere fancy or caprice. Our dictionaries, by a strange oversight or negligence, do not recognize them as words; and writers have in general spelled them with very little regard to either authority or analogy. What they are, or ought to be, has therefore been treated as a trifling question: and, what is still more surprising, several authors of spelling-books make no mention at all of them; while others, here at the very threshold of instruction, teach falsely—giving "he" for *Aitch,* "er" for *Ar,* "oo" or "uu" for *Double-u,* "ye" for *Wy,* and writing almost all the rest improperly. So that many persons who think themselves well educated, would be greatly puzzled to name on paper these simple elements of all learning. Nay, there can be found a hundred men who can readily write the alphabetic names which were in use two or three thousand years ago in Greece or Palestine, for one who can do the same thing with propriety, respecting those which we now employ so constantly in English: [88] and yet the words themselves are as familiar to every school-boy's lips as are the characters to his eye. This fact may help to convince us, that *the grammar* of our language has never yet been sufficiently taught. Among all the particulars which constitute this subject, there are none which better deserve to be everywhere known, by proper and determinate names, than these prime elements of all written language.

OBS. 4.—Should it happen to be asked a hundred lustrums hence, what were the names of the letters in "the Augustan age of English literature," or in the days of William the Fourth and Andrew Jackson, I fear the learned of that day will be as much at a loss for an answer, as would most of our college tutors now, were they asked, by what series of names the Roman youth were taught to spell. Might not Quintilian or Varro have obliged many, by recording these? As it is, we are indebted to Priscian, a grammarian of the sixth century, for almost all we know about them. But even the information which may be had, on this point, has been strangely overlooked by our common Latin grammarians.[89] What, but the greater care of earlier writers, has made the Greek names better known or more important than the Latin? In every nation that is not totally illiterate, custom must have established for the letters a certain set of names, which are *the only true ones*, and which are of course to be preferred to such as are local or unauthorized. In this, however, as in other things, use may sometimes vary, and possibly improve; but when its decisions are clear, no feeble reason should be allowed to disturb them. Every parent, therefore, who would have his children instructed to read and write the English language, should see that in the first place they learn to name the letters as they are commonly named in English. A Scotch gentleman of good education informs me, that the names of the letters, as he first learned them in a school in his own country, were these: "A, Ib, Ec, Id, E, Iff, Ig, Ich, I, Ij, Ik, Ill, Im, In, O, Ip, Kue, Ir, Iss, It, U, Iv, Double-u, Ix, Wy, Iz;" but that in the same school the English names are now used. It is to be hoped, that all teachers will in time abandon every such local usage, and name the letters *as they ought to be named*; and that the day will come, in which the regular English *orthography* of these terms, shall be steadily preferred, ignorance of it be thought a disgrace, and the makers of school-books feel no longer at liberty to alter names that are a thousand times better known than their own.

OBS. 5.—It is not in respect to their *orthography* alone, that these first words in literature demand inquiry and reflection: the *pronunciation* of some of them has often been taught erroneously, and, with respect to three or four of them, some writers have attempted to make an entire change from the customary forms which I have recorded. Whether the name of the first letter should be pronounced "*Aye*," as it is in England, "*Ah*," as it is in

Ireland, or "*Aw*," as it is in Scotland, is a question which Walker has largely discussed, and clearly decided in favour of the first sound; and this decision accords with the universal practice of the schools in America. It is remarkable that this able critic, though he treated minutely of the letters, naming them all in the outset of his "Principles" subsequently neglected the names of them all, except the first and the last. Of *Zee*, (which has also been called *Zed, Zad, Izzard, Uzzard, Izzet,* and *Iz,*)[90] he says, "Its common name is *izzard*, which Dr. Johnson explains into *s hard*; if, however, this is the meaning, it is a gross misnomer; for the *z* is not the hard, but the soft *s*; [91] but as it has a less sharp, and therefore not so audible a sound, it is not impossible *but* it may mean *s surd. Zed,* borrowed from the French, is the more fashionable name of this letter; but, in my opinion, *not to be admitted, because the names of the letters ought to have no diversity.*"—*Walker's Principles*, No. 483. It is true, the name of a letter ought to be one, and in no respect diverse; but where diversity has already obtained, and become firmly rooted in custom, is it to be obviated by insisting upon what is old-fashioned, awkward, and inconvenient? Shall the better usage give place to the worse? Uniformity cannot be so reached. In this country, both *Zed* and *Izzard*, as well as the worse forms *Zad* and *Uzzard*, are now fairly superseded by the softer and better term *Zee*; and whoever will spell aloud, with each of these names, a few such words as *dizzy, mizzen, gizzard,* may easily perceive why none of the former can ever be brought again into use. The other two, *Iz* and *Izzet*, being localisms, and not authorized English, I give up all six; *Zed* to the French, and the rest to oblivion.

OBS. 6.—By way of apology for noticing the name of the first letter, Walker observes, "If a diversity of names to vowels did not confound us in our spelling, or declaring to each other the component letters of a word, it would be entirely needless to enter into *so trifling a question* as the mere name of a letter; but when we find ourselves unable to convey signs to each other on account of this diversity of names, and that words themselves are endangered by an improper utterance of their component parts, it seems highly incumbent on us to attempt a uniformity in this point, which, insignificant as it may seem, is undoubtedly the foundation of a just and regular pronunciation."—*Dict., under A.* If diversity in this matter is so perplexing, what shall we say to those who are attempting innovations without assigning reasons, or even pretending authority? and if a knowledge of these names is the basis of a just pronunciation, what shall we think of him who will take no pains to ascertain how he ought to speak and write them? He who pretends to teach the proper fashion of speaking and writing, cannot deal honestly, if ever he silently prefer a suggested improvement, to any established and undisturbed usage of the language; for, in grammar, no individual authority can be a counterpoise to general custom. The best usage can never be that which is little known, nor can it be well ascertained and taught by him who knows little. Inquisitive minds are ever curious to learn the nature, origin, and causes of things; and that instruction is the most useful, which is best calculated to gratify this rational curiosity. This is my apology for dwelling so long upon the present topic.

OBS. 7.—The names originally given to the letters were not mere notations of sound, intended solely to express or make known the powers of the several characters then in use; nor ought even the modern names of our present letters, though formed with special reference to their sounds, to be considered such. Expressions of mere sound, such as the notations in a pronouncing dictionary, having no reference to what is meant by the sound, do not constitute words at all; because they are not those acknowledged signs to which a meaning has been attached, and are consequently without that significance which is an essential property of words. But, in every language, there must be a series of sounds by which the alphabetical characters are commonly known in speech; and which, as they are the acknowledged names of these particular objects, must be entitled to a place among *the words* of the language. It is a great error to judge otherwise; and a greater to make it a "trifling question" in grammar, whether a given letter shall be called by one name or by an other. Who shall say that *Daleth*, *Delta*, and *Dee*, are not three *real words*, each equally important in the language to which it properly belongs? Such names have always been in use wherever literature has been cultivated; and as the forms and powers of the letters have been changed by the nations, and have become different in different languages, there has necessarily followed a change of the names. For, whatever inconvenience scholars may find in the diversity which has thence arisen, to name these elements in a set of foreign terms, inconsistent with the genius of the language to be learned, would surely be attended with a tenfold greater. We derived our letters, and their names too, from the Romans; but this is no good reason why the latter should be spelled and pronounced as we suppose they were spelled and pronounced in Rome.

OBS. 8.—The names of the twenty-two letters in Hebrew, are, without dispute, proper *words*; for they are not only significant of the letters thus named, but have in general, if not in every instance, some other meaning in that language. Thus the mysterious ciphers which the English reader meets with, and wonders over, as he reads the 119th Psalm, may be resolved, according to some of the Hebrew grammars, as follows:—

[Hebrew: Aleph] Aleph, A, an ox, or a leader; [Hebrew: Beth] Beth, Bee, house; [Hebrew: Gimel] Gimel, Gee, a camel; [Hebrew: Dalet] Daleth, Dee, a door; [Hebrew: he] He, E, she, or behold; [Hebrew: vav] Vau, U, a hook, or a nail; [Hebrew: zajin] Zain, Zee, armour; [Hebrew: het] Cheth, or Heth, Aitch, a hedge; [Hebrew: tet] Teth, Tee, a serpent, or a scroll; [Hebrew: jod] Jod, or Yod, I, or Wy, a hand shut; [Hebrew: kaf] Caph, Cee, a hollow hand, or a cup; [Hebrew: lamed] Lamed, Ell, an ox-goad; [Hebrew: mem] Mem, Em, a stain, or spot; [Hebrew: nun] Nun, En, a fish, or a snake; [Hebrew: samekh] Samech, Ess, a basis, or support; [Hebrew: ayin] Ain, or Oin, O, an eye, or a well; [Hebrew: pe] Pe, Pee, a lip, or mouth; [Hebrew: tsadi]

Tzaddi, or Tsadhe, Tee-zee, (i. e. tz, or ts,) a hunter's pole; [Hebrew: qof] Koph, Kue, or Kay, an ape; [Hebrew: resh] Resch, or Resh, Ar, a head; [Hebrew: shin] Schin, or Sin, Ess-aitch, or Ess, a tooth; [Hebrew: tav] Tau, or Thau, Tee, or Tee-aitch, a cross, or mark.

These English names of the Hebrew letters are written with much less uniformity than those of the Greek, because there has been more dispute respecting their powers. This is directly contrary to what one would have expected; since the Hebrew names are words originally significant of other things than the letters, and the Greek are not. The original pronunciation of both languages is admitted to be lost, or involved in so much obscurity that little can be positively affirmed about it; and yet, where least was known, grammarians have produced the most diversity; aiming at disputed sounds in the one case, but generally preferring a correspondence of letters in the other.

OBS. 9.—The word *alphabet* is derived from the first two names in the following series. The Greek letters are twenty-four; which are formed, named, and sounded, thus:—

[Greek: A a], Alpha, a; [Greek: B, b], Beta, b; [Greek: G g], Gamma, g hard; [Greek: D d], Delta, d; [Greek: E e], Epsilon, e short; [Greek: Z z], Zeta, z; [Greek: Æ æ], Eta, e long; [Greek: TH Th th], Theta, th; [Greek: I i], Iota, i; [Greek K k], Kappa, k; [Greek: L l], Lambda, l; [Greek: M m], Mu, m; [Greek: N n], Nu, n; [Greek: X x], Xi, x; [Greek: O o], Omicron, o short; [Greek: P p], Pi, p; [Greek: R r] Rho, r; [Greek: S s s], Sigma, s; [Greek: T t], Tau, t; [Greek: Y y], Upsilon, u; [Greek: PH ph], Phi, ph; [Greek: CH ch], Chi, ch; [Greek: PS ps], Psi, ps; [Greek: O o], Omega, o long.

Of these names, our English dictionaries explain the first and the last; and Webster has defined *Iota*, and *Zeta*, but without reference to the meaning of the former in Greek. *Beta, Delta, Lambda,* and perhaps some others, are also found in the etymologies or definitions of Johnson and Webster, both of whom spell the word *Lambda* and its derivative *lambdoidal* without the silent *b,* which is commonly, if not always, inserted by the authors of our Greek grammars, and which Worcester, more properly, retains.

OBS. 10.—The reader will observe that the foregoing names, whether Greek or Hebrew, are in general much less simple than those which our letters now bear; and if he has ever attempted to spell aloud in either of those languages, he cannot but be sensible of the great advantage which was gained when to each letter there was given a short name, expressive, as ours mostly are, of its ordinary power. This improvement appears to have been introduced by the Romans, whose names for the letters were even more simple than our own. But so negligent in respect to them have been the Latin grammarians, both ancient and modern, that few even of the learned can tell what they really were in that language; or how they differed, either in orthography or sound, from those of the English or the French, the Hebrew or the Greek. Most of them, however, may yet be ascertained from Priscian, and some others of note among the ancient philologists; so that by taking from later authors the names of those letters which were not used in old times, we can still furnish an entire list, concerning the accuracy of which there is not much room to dispute. It is probable that in the ancient pronunciation of Latin, *a* was commonly sounded as in *father;* *e* like the English *a; i* mostly like *e* long; *y* like *i* short; *c* generally and *g* always hard, as in *come* and *go.* But, as the original, native, or just pronunciation of a language is not necessary to an understanding of it when written, the existing nations have severally, in a great measure, accommodated themselves, in their manner of reading this and other ancient tongues.

OBS. 11.—As the Latin language is now printed, its letters are twenty-five. Like the French, it has all that belong to the English alphabet, except the *Double-u*. But, till the first Punic war, the Romans wrote C for G, and doubtless gave it the power as well as the place of the Gamma or Gimel. It then seems to have slid into K; but they used it also for S, as we do now. The ancient Saxons, generally pronounced C as K, but sometimes as Ch. Their G was either guttural, or like our Y. In some of the early English grammars the name of the latter is written *Ghee*. The letter F, when first invented, was called, from its shape, Digamma, and afterwards Ef. J, when it was first distinguished from I, was called by the Hebrew name Jod, and afterwards Je. V, when first distinguished from U, was called Vau, then Va, then Ve. Y, when the Romans first borrowed it from the Greeks, was called Ypsilon; and Z, from the same source, was called Zeta; and, as these two letters were used only in words of Greek origin, I know not whether they ever received from the Romans any shorter names. In Schneider's Latin Grammar, the letters are named in the following manner; except Je and Ve, which are omitted by this author: "A, Be, Ce, De, E, Ef, Ge, Ha, I, [Je,] Ka, El, Em, En, O, Pe, Cu, Er, Es, Te, U, [Ve,] Ix, Ypsilon, Zeta." And this I suppose to be the most proper way of writing their names *in Latin*, unless we have sufficient authority for shortening Ypsilon into Y, sounded as short *i*, and for changing Zeta into Ez.

OBS. 12.—In many, if not in all languages, the five vowels, A, E, I, O, U, name themselves; but they name themselves differently to the ear, according to the different ways of uttering them in different languages. And as the name of a consonant necessarily requires one or more vowels, that also may be affected in the same manner. But in every language there should be a known way both of writing and of speaking every name in the series; and that, if there is nothing to hinder, should be made conformable to *the genius of the language*. I do not say that the names above can be regularly declined in Latin; but in English it is as easy to speak of two Dees as of two trees, of two Kays as of two days, of two Exes as of two foxes, of two Effs as of two skiffs; and there ought to be no more difficulty about the correct way of writing the word in the one case, than in the other. In Dr. Sam. Prat's Latin Grammar, (an elaborate octavo, all Latin, published in London, 1722,) nine of the consonants are reckoned mutes; b, c, d, g, p, q, t, j, and v; and eight, semivowels; f, l, m, n, r, s, x, z. "All the mutes," says this author, "are named by placing *e* after them; as, be, ce, de, ge, except *q*, which ends in *u*." See p. 8. "The semivowels, beginning with *e*, end in themselves; as, ef, *ach*, el, em, en, er, es, *ex*, (or, as Priscian will have it, *ix*,) *eds*." See p. 9. This mostly accords with the names given in the preceding paragraph; and so far as it does not, I judge the author to be wrong. The reader will observe that the Doctor's explanation is neither very exact nor quite complete: K is a mute which is not enumerated, and the rule would make the name of it *Ke*, and not *Ka*;—H is not one of his eight semivowels, nor does the name Ach accord with his rule or seem like a Latin word;—the name of Z, according to his principle, would be *Ez* and not "*Eds*," although the latter may better indicate the *sound* which was then given to this letter.

OBS. 13.—If the history of these names exhibits diversity, so does that of almost all other terms; and yet there is some way of writing every word with correctness, and correctness tends to permanence. But Time, that establishes authority, destroys it also, when he fairly sanctions newer customs. To all names worthy to be known, it is natural to wish a perpetual uniformity; but if any one thinks the variableness of these to be peculiar, let him open the English Bible of the fourteenth century, and read a few verses, observing the names. For instance: "Forsothe whanne *Eroude* was to bringynge forth hym, in that nigt *Petir* was slepynge bitwixe tweyno knytis."—*Dedis*, (i. e., *Acts*,) xii, 6. "*Crist Ihesu* that is to demynge the quyke and deed."—*2 Tim.*, iv, 1. Since this was written for English, our language has changed much, and at the same time acquired, by means of the press, some aids to stability. I have recorded above the *true* names of the letters, as they are now used, with something of their history; and if there could be in human works any thing unchangeable, I should wish, (with due deference to all schemers and fault-finders,) that these names might remain the same forever.

OBS. 14.—If any change is desirable in our present names of the letters, it is that we may have a shorter and simpler term in stead of *Double-u*. But can we change this well known name? I imagine it would be about as easy to change *Alpha, Upsilon, or Omega*; and perhaps it would be as useful. Let Dr. Webster, or any defender of his spelling, try it. He never named the *English* letters rightly; long ago discarded the term *Double-u*; and is not yet tired of his experiment with "*oo*;" but thinks still to make the vowel sound of this letter its name. Yet he writes his new name wrong; has no authority for it but his own; and is, most certainly, reprehensible for the *innovation*. [92] If W is to be named as a vowel, it ought to *name itself*, as other vowels do, and not to take *two Oes* for its written name. Who that knows what it is, to name a letter, can think of naming *w* by double *o*? That it is possible for an ingenious man to misconceive this simple affair of naming the letters, may appear not only from the foregoing instance, but from the following quotation: "Among the thousand mismanagements of literary instruction, there is at the outset in the hornbook, *the pretence to represent elementary sounds* by syllables composed of two or more elements; as, *Be, Kay, Zed, Double-u,* and *Aitch*. These words are used in infancy, and through life, as *simple elements* in the process of synthetic spelling. If the definition of a *consonant* was made by the master from the practice of the child, it might suggest pity for the pedagogue, but should not make us forget the realities of nature."—*Dr. Push, on the Philosophy of the Human Voice*, p. 52. This is a strange allegation to come from such a source. If I bid a boy spell the word *why*, he says, "Double-u, Aitch, Wy, *hwi*;" and knows that he has spelled and pronounced the word correctly. But if he conceives that the five syllables which form the three words, *Double-u,* and *Aitch,* and *Wy*, are the three simple sounds which he utters in pronouncing the word *why*, it is not because the hornbook, or the teacher of the hornbook, ever made any such blunder or "pretence;" but because, like some great philosophers, he is capable of misconceiving very plain things. Suppose he should take it into his head to follow Dr. Webster's books, and to say, "Oo, he, ye, *hwi*;" who, but these doctors, would imagine, that such spelling was supported either by "the realities of nature," or by the authority of custom? I shall retain both the old "definition of a consonant," and the usual names of the letters, notwithstanding the contemptuous pity it may excite in the minds of *such* critics.

II.CLASSESOFTHELETTERS.

The letters are divided into two general classes, *vowels* and *consonants*.

A *vowel* is a letter which forms a perfect sound when uttered alone; as, *a, e, o.*

A *consonant* is a letter which cannot be perfectly uttered till joined to a vowel; as, *b, c, d.*[93]

The vowels are *a, e, i, o, u,* and sometimes *w* and *y.* All the other letters are consonants.

W or *y* is called a consonant when it precedes a vowel heard in the same syllable; as in *wine, twine, whine; ye, yet, youth*: in all other cases, these letters are vowels; as in *Yssel, Ystadt, yttria; newly, dewy, eyebrow.*

CLASSESOFCONSONANTS.

The consonants are divided, with respect to their powers, into *semivowels* and *mutes.*

A *semivowel* is a consonant which can be imperfectly sounded without a vowel, so that at the end of a syllable its sound may be protracted; as, *l, n, z,* in *al, an, az.*

A *mute* is a consonant which cannot be sounded at all without a vowel, and which at the end of a syllable suddenly stops the breath; as, *k, p, t,* in *ak, ap, at.*

The semivowels are, *f, h, j, l, m, n, r, s, v, w, x, y, z,* and *c* and *g* soft: but *w* or *y* at the end of a syllable, is a vowel; and the sound of *c, f, g, h, j, s,* or *x,* can be protracted only as an *aspirate,* or strong breath.

Four of the semivowels,—*l, m, n,* and *r,*—are termed *liquids,* on account of the fluency of their sounds; and four others,—*v, w, y,* and *z,*—are likewise more vocal than the aspirates.

The mutes are eight;—*b, d, k, p, q, t,* and *c* and *g* hard: three of these,—*k, q,* and *c* hard,—sound exactly alike: *b, d,* and *g* hard, stop the voice less suddenly than the rest.

OBSERVATIONS.

OBS. 1.—The foregoing division of the letters is of very great antiquity, and, in respect to its principal features sanctioned by almost universal authority; yet if we examine it minutely, either with reference to the various opinions of the learned, or with regard to the essential differences among the things of which it speaks, it will not perhaps be found in all respects indisputably certain. It will however be of use, as a basis for some subsequent rules, and as a means of calling the attention of the learner to the manner in which he utters the sounds of the letters. A knowledge of about three dozen different elementary sounds is implied in the faculty of speech. The power of producing these sounds with distinctness, and of adapting them to the purposes for which language is used, constitutes perfection of utterance. Had we a perfect alphabet, consisting of one symbol, and only one, for each elementary sound; and a perfect method of spelling, freed from silent letters, and precisely adjusted to the most correct pronunciation of words; the process of learning to read would doubtless be greatly facilitated. And yet any attempt toward such a reformation, any change short of the introduction of some entirely new mode of writing, would be both unwise and impracticable. It would involve our laws and literature in utter confusion, because pronunciation is the least permanent part of language; and if the orthography of words were conformed entirely to this standard, their origin and meaning would, in many instances, be soon lost. We must therefore content ourselves to learn languages as they are, and to make the best use we can of our present imperfect system of alphabetic characters; and we may be the better satisfied to do this, because the deficiencies and redundancies of this alphabet are not yet so well ascertained, as to make it certain what a perfect one would be.

OBS. 2.—In order to have a right understanding of the letters, it is necessary to enumerate, as accurately as we can, the elementary *sounds* of the language; and to attend carefully to the manner in which these sounds are enunciated, as well as to the characters by which they are represented. The most unconcerned observer cannot but perceive that there are certain differences in the sounds, as well as in the shapes, of the letters; and yet under what heads they ought severally to be classed, or how many of them will fall under some particular name, it may occasionally puzzle a philosopher to tell. The student must consider what is proposed or asked, use his own senses, and judge for himself. With our lower-case alphabet before him, he can tell by his own eye, which are the long letters, and which the short ones; so let him learn by his own ear, which are the vowels, and which, the consonants. The processes are alike simple; and, if he be neither blind nor deaf, he can do both about equally well. Thus he may know for a certainty, that *a* is a short letter, and *b* a long one; the former a vowel, the latter a consonant: and so of others. Yet as he may doubt whether *t* is a long letter or a short one, so he may be puzzled to say whether *w* and *y*, as heard in *we* and *ye*, are vowels or consonants: but neither of these difficulties should impair his confidence in any of his other decisions. If he attain by observation and practice a clear and perfect pronunciation of the letters, he will be able to class them for himself with as much accuracy as he will find in books.

OBS. 3.—Grammarians have generally agreed that every letter is either a vowel or a consonant; and also that there are among the latter some semivowels, some mutes, some aspirates, some liquids, some sharps, some flats, some labials, some dentals, some nasals, some palatals, and perhaps yet other species; but in enumerating the letters which belong to these several classes, they disagree so much as to make it no easy matter to ascertain what particular classification is best supported by their authority. I have adopted what I conceive to be the best authorized, and at the same time the most intelligible. He that dislikes the scheme, may do better, if he can. But let him with modesty determine what sort of discoveries may render our ancient authorities questionable. Aristotle, three hundred and thirty years before Christ, divided the Greek letters into *vowels, semivowels*, and *mutes*, and declared that no syllable could be formed without a vowel. In the opinion of some neoterics, it has been reserved to our age, to detect the fallacy of this. But I would fain believe that the Stagirite knew as well what he was saying, as did Dr. James Rush, when, in 1827, he declared the doctrine of vowels and consonants to be "a misrepresentation." The latter philosopher resolves the letters into "*tonics, subtonics*, and *atonics*;" and avers that "consonants alone may form syllables." Indeed, I cannot but think the ancient doctrine better. For, to say that "consonants alone may form syllables," is as much as to say that consonants are not consonants, but vowels! To be consistent, the attempters of this reformation should never speak of vowels or consonants, semivowels or mutes; because they judge the terms inappropriate, and the classification absurd. They should therefore adhere strictly to their "tonics, subtonics, and atonics;" which classes, though apparently the same as vowels, semivowels, and mutes, are better adapted to their new and peculiar division of these elements. Thus, by reforming both language and philosophy at once, they may make what they will of either!

OBS. 4.—Some teach that *w* and *y* are always vowels: conceiving the former to be equivalent to *oo*, and the latter to *i* or *e*. Dr. Lowth says, "*Y* is always a vowel," and "*W* is either a vowel or a diphthong." Dr. Webster supposes *w* to be always "a vowel, a simple sound;" but admits that, "At the beginning of words, *y* is called an *articulation* or *consonant*, and *with some propriety perhaps*, as it brings the root of the tongue in close contact with the lower part of the palate, and nearly in the position to which the close *g* brings it."—*American Dict., Octavo*. But I follow Wallis, Brightland, Johnson, Walker, Murray, Worcester, and others, in considering both of them sometimes vowels and sometimes consonants. They are consonants at the beginning of words in English, because their sounds take the article *a*, and not *an*, before them; as, *a wall, a yard*, and not, *an wall, an yard*. But *oo* or the sound of *e*, requires *an*, and not *a*; as, *an eel, an oozy bog*.[94] At the end of a syllable we know they are vowels; but at the beginning, they are so squeezed in their pronunciation, as to follow a vowel without any hiatus, or difficulty of utterance; as, "*O worthy youth! so young, so wise!*"

OBS. 5.—Murray's rule, "*W* and *y* are consonants when they begin a word or syllable, but in every other situation they are vowels," which is found in Comly's book, *Kirkham's*, Merchant's, Ingersoll's, Fisk's. Hart's, Hiley's, Alger's, Bullions's, Pond's, S. Putnam's, Weld's, and in sundry other grammars, is favourable to my doctrine, but too badly conceived to be quoted here as authority. It *undesignedly* makes *w* a consonant in *wine*, and a vowel in *twine*; and *y* a consonant when it *forms* a syllable, as in *dewy*: for a letter that *forms* a syllable, "begins" it. But *Kirkham* has lately learned his letters anew; and, supposing he had Dr. Rush on his side, has philosophically taken their names for their sounds. He now calls *y* a "*diphthong.*" But he is wrong here by his own showing: he should rather have called it a *triphthong*. He says, "By pronouncing in a very deliberate and perfectly natural manner, the letter *y*, (which is a *diphthong*,) the *unpractised* student will perceive, that the sound produced, is compound; being formed, at its opening, of the obscure sound of *oo* as heard in *oo*-ze, which sound rapidly slides into that of *i*, and then advances to that of *ee* as heard in *e*-ve, *and* on which it gradually passes off into silence."—*Kirkham's Elocution*, p. 75. Thus the "unpractised student" is taught that *b-y* spells *bwy*; or, if pronounced "very deliberately, *boo-i-ee*!" Nay, this grammatist makes *b*, not a labial mute, as Walker, Webster, Cobb, and others, have called it, but a nasal subtonic, or semivowel. He delights in protracting its "guttural murmur;" perhaps, in assuming its name for its sound; and, having proved, that "consonants are capable of forming syllables," finds no difficulty in mouthing this little monosyllable *by* into *b-oo-i-ee!* In this way, it is the easiest thing in the world, for such a man to outface Aristotle, or any other divider of the letters; for he *makes* the sounds by which he judges. "Boy," says the teacher of Kirkham's Elocution, "describe the protracted sound of *y*."—*Kirkham's Elocution*, p. 110. The pupil may answer, "That letter, sir, has no longer or more complex sound, than what is heard in the word *eye*, or in the vowel *i*; but the book which I study, describes it otherwise. I know not whether I can make you understand it, but I will *tr-oo-i-ee*." If the word *try*, which the author uses as an example, does not exhibit his "protracted sound of *y*," there is no word that does: the sound is a mere fiction, originating in strange ignorance.

OBS. 6.—In the large print above, I have explained the principal classes of the letters, but not all that are spoken of in books. It is proper to inform the learner that the *sharp* consonants are *t*, and all others after which our contracted preterits and participles require that *d* should be sounded like *t*; as in the words faced, reached, stuffed, laughed, triumphed, croaked, cracked, houghed, reaped, nipped, piqued, missed, wished, earthed, betrothed, fixed. The *flat* or *smooth* consonants are *d*, and all others with which the proper sound of *d* may be united; as in the words, daubed, judged, hugged, thronged, sealed, filled, aimed, crammed, pained, planned, feared, marred, soothed, loved, dozed, buzzed. The *labials* are those consonants which are articulated chiefly by the lips; among which, Dr. Webster reckons *b*, *f*, *m*, *p*, and *v*. But Dr. Rush says, *b* and *m* are nasals, the latter, "purely nasal." [95] The *dentals* are those consonants which are referred to the teeth; the *nasals* are those which are affected by the nose; and the *palatals* are those which compress the palate, as *k* and hard *g*. But these last-named classes are not of much importance; nor have I thought it worth while to notice *minutely* the opinions of writers respecting the others, as whether *h* is a semivowel, or a mute, or neither.

OBS. 7.—The Cherokee alphabet, which was invented in 1821, by See-quo-yah, or George Guess, an ingenious but wholly illiterate Indian, contains eighty-five letters, or characters. But the sounds of the language are much fewer than ours; for the characters represent, not simple tones and articulations, but *syllabic sounds*, and this number is said to be sufficient to denote them all. But the different syllabic sounds in our language amount to some thousands. I suppose, from the account, that *See-quo-yah* writes his name, in his own language, with three letters; and that characters so used, would not require, and probably would not admit, such a division as that of vowels and consonants. One of the Cherokees, in a letter to the American Lyceum, states, that a knowledge of this mode of writing is so easily acquired, that one who understands and speaks the language, "can learn to read in a day; and, indeed," continues the writer, "I have known some to acquire the art in a single evening. It is only necessary to learn the different sounds of the characters, to be enabled to read at once. In the English language, we must not only first learn the letters, but to spell, before reading; but in Cherokee, all that is required, is, to learn the letters; for they have *syllabic sounds*, and by connecting different ones together, a word is formed: in which there is no art. All who understand the language can do so, and both read and write, so soon as they can learn to trace with their fingers the forms of the characters. I suppose that more than one half of the Cherokees can read their own language, and are thereby enabled to acquire much valuable information, with which they otherwise would never have been blessed."—*W. S. Coodey*, 1831.

OBS. 8.—From the foregoing account, it would appear that the Cherokee language is a very peculiar one: its words must either be very few, or the proportion of polysyllables very great. The characters used in China and Japan, stand severally for *words*; and their number is said to be not less than seventy thousand; so that the study of a whole life is scarcely sufficient to make a man thoroughly master of them. Syllabic writing is represented by Dr. Blair as a great improvement upon the Chinese method, and yet as being far inferior to that which is properly *alphabetic*, like ours. "The first step, in this new progress," says he, "was the invention of an alphabet of syllables, which probably preceded the invention of an alphabet of letters, among some of the ancient nations; and which is said to be retained to this day, in Ethiopia, and some countries of India. By fixing upon a particular mark, or character, for every syllable in the language, the number of characters, necessary to be used in writing, was reduced within a much smaller compass than the number of words in the language. Still, however, the number of characters was great; and must have continued to render both reading and writing very laborious arts. Till, at last, some happy genius arose, and tracing the sounds made by the human voice, to their most simple elements, reduced them to a very few *vowels and consonants*; and, by affixing to each of these, the signs which we now call letters, taught men how, by their combinations, to put in writing all the different words, or combinations of sound, which they employed in speech. By being reduced to this simplicity, the art of writing was brought to its highest state of perfection; and, in this state, we now enjoy it in all the countries of Europe."—*Blair's Rhetoric*, Lect. VII, p. 68.

OBS. 9.—All certain knowledge of the sounds given to the letters by Moses and the prophets having been long ago lost, a strange dispute has arisen, and been carried on for centuries, concerning this question, "Whether the Hebrew letters are, or are not, *all consonants*:" the vowels being supposed by some to be suppressed and understood; and not written, except by *points* of comparatively late invention. The discussion of such a question does not properly belong to English grammar; but, on account of its curiosity, as well as of its analogy to some of our present disputes, I mention it. Dr. Charles Wilson says, "After we have sufficiently known the figures and names of the letters, the next step is, to learn to enunciate or to pronounce them, so as to produce articulate sounds. On this subject, which appears at first sight very plain and simple, numberless contentions and varieties of opinion meet us at the threshold. From the earliest period of the invention of written characters to represent human language, however more or less remote that time may be, it seems absolutely certain, that the distinction of letters into *vowels and consonants* must have obtained. All the speculations of the Greek grammarians assume this as a first principle." Again: "I beg leave only to premise this observation, that I absolutely and unequivocally deny the position, that all the letters of the Hebrew alphabet are consonants; and, after the most careful and minute inquiry, give it as my opinion, that of the twenty-two letters of which the Hebrew alphabet consists, five are vowels and seventeen are consonants. The five vowels by name are, Aleph, He, Vau, Yod, and Ain."—*Wilson's Heb. Gram.*, pp. 6 and 8.

III. POWERS OF THE LETTERS.

The powers of the letters are properly those elementary sounds which their figures are used to represent; but letters formed into words, are capable of communicating thought independently of sound. The simple elementary sounds of any language are few, commonly not more than *thirty-six*;[96] but they may be variously *combined*, so as to form words innumerable. Different vowel sounds, or vocal elements, are produced by opening the mouth differently, and placing the tongue in a peculiar manner for each; but the voice may vary in loudness, pitch, or time, and still utter the same vowel power.

The *vowel sounds* which form the basis of the English language, and which ought therefore to be perfectly familiar to every one who speaks it, are those which are heard at the beginning of the words, *ate, at, ah, all, eel, ell, isle, ill, old, on, ooze, use, us*, and that of *u* in *bull*.

In the formation of syllables, some of these fourteen primary sounds may be joined together, as in *ay, oil, out, owl*; and all of them may be preceded or followed by certain motions and positions of the lips and tongue, which will severally convert them into other terms in speech. Thus the same essential sounds may be changed into a new series of words by an *f*; as, *fate, fat, far, fall, feel, fell, file, fill, fold, fond, fool, fuse, fuss, full*. Again, into as many more with a *p*; as, *pate, pat, par, pall, peel, pell, pile, pill, pole, pond, pool, pule, purl, pull.* Each of the vowel sounds may be variously expressed by letters. About half of them are sometimes words: the rest are seldom, if ever, used alone even to form syllables. But the reader may easily learn to utter them all, separately, according to the foregoing series. Let us note them as plainly as possible: eigh, ~a, ah, awe, =eh, ~e, eye, ~i, oh, ~o, oo, yew, ~u, û. Thus the eight long sounds, *eigh, ah, awe, eh, eye, oh, ooh, yew,* are, or may be, words; but the six less vocal, called the short vowel sounds, as in *at, et, it, ot, ut, put,* are commonly heard only in connexion with consonants; except the first, which is perhaps the most frequent sound of the vowel A or *a*—a sound sometimes given to the word *a*, perhaps most generally; as in the phrase, "twice ~*a* day."

The simple *consonant sounds* in English are twenty-two: they are marked by *b, d, f, g hard, h, k, l, m, n, ng, p, r, s, sh, t, th sharp, th flat, v, w, y, z,* and *zh*. But *zh* is written only to show the sound of other letters; as of *s* in *pleasure,* or *z* in *azure.*

All these sounds are heard distinctly in the following words: *buy, die, fie, guy, high, kie, lie, my, nigh, eying, pie, rye, sigh, shy, tie, thigh, thy, vie, we, ye, zebra, seizure.* Again: most of them may be repeated in the same word, if not in the same syllable; as in *bibber, diddle, fifty, giggle, high-hung, cackle, lily, mimic, ninny, singing, pippin, mirror, hissest, flesh-brush, tittle, thinketh, thither, vivid, witwal, union,*[97] *dizzies, vision.*

With us, the consonants J and X represent, not simple, but complex sounds: hence they are never doubled. J is equivalent to *dzh*; and X, either to *ks* or to *gz*. The former ends no English word, and the latter begins none. To the initial X of foreign words, we always give the simple sound of Z; as in *Xerxes, xebec.*

The consonants C and Q have no sounds peculiar to themselves. Q has always the power of *k*. C is hard, like *k*, before *a, o,* and *u*; and soft, like *s,* before *e, i,* and *y*: thus the syllables, *ca, ce, ci, co, cu, cy,* are pronounced, *ka, se, si, ko, ku, sy*. S before *c* preserves the former sound, but coalesces with the latter; hence the syllables, *sca, sce, sci, sco, scu, scy,* are sounded, *ska, se, si, sko, sku, sy*. *Ce* and *ci* have sometimes the sound of *sh*; as in *ocean, social. Ch* commonly represents the compound sound of *tsh*; as in *church*.

G, as well as C, has different sounds before different vowels. G is always hard, or guttural, before *a, o,* and *u*; and generally soft, like *j*, before *e, i,* or *y*: thus the syllables, *ga, ge, gi, go, gu, gy,* are pronounced *ga, je, ji, go, gu, jy*.

The possible combinations and mutations of the twenty-six letters of our alphabet, are many millions of millions. But those clusters which are unpronounceable, are useless. Of such as may be easily uttered, there are more than enough for all the purposes of useful writing, or the recording of speech.

Thus it is, that from principles so few and simple as about six or seven and thirty plain elementary sounds, represented by characters still fewer, we derive such a variety of oral and written signs, as may suffice to explain or record all the sentiments and transactions of all men in all ages.

OBSERVATIONS.

OBS. 1.—A knowledge of sounds can be acquired, in the first instance, only by the ear. No description of the manner of their production, or of the differences which distinguish them, can be at all intelligible to him who has not already, by the sense of hearing, acquired a knowledge of both. What I here say of the sounds of the letters, must of course be addressed to those persons only who are able both to speak and to read English. Why then attempt instruction by a method which both ignorance and knowledge on the part of the pupil, must alike render useless? I have supposed some readers to have such an acquaintance with the powers of the letters, as is but loose and imperfect; sufficient for the accurate pronunciation of some words or syllables, but leaving them liable to mistakes in others; extending perhaps to all the sounds of the language, but not to a ready analysis or enumeration of them. Such persons may profit by a written description of the powers of the letters, though no such description can equal the clear impression of the living voice. Teachers, too, whose business it is to aid the articulation of the young, and, by a patient inculcation of elementary principles, to lay the foundation of an accurate pronunciation, may derive some assistance from any notation of these principles, which will help their memory, or that of the learner. The connexion between letters and sounds is altogether *arbitrary*; but a few positions, being assumed and made known, in respect to some characters, become easy standards for further instruction in respect to others of similar sound.

OBS. 2.—The importance of being instructed at an early age, to pronounce with distinctness and facility all the elementary sounds of one's native language, has been so frequently urged, and is so obvious in itself, that none but those who have been themselves neglected, will be likely to disregard the claims of their children in this respect.[98] But surely an accurate knowledge of the ordinary powers of the letters would be vastly more common, were there not much hereditary negligence respecting the manner in which these important rudiments are learned. The utterance of the illiterate may exhibit wit and native talent, but it is always more or less barbarous, because it is not aided by a knowledge of orthography. For pronunciation and orthography, however they may seem, in our language especially, to be often at variance, are certainly correlative: a true knowledge of either tends to the preservation of both. Each of the letters represents some one or more of the elementary sounds, exclusive of the rest; and each of the elementary sounds, though several of them are occasionally transferred, has some one or two letters to which it most properly or most frequently belongs. But borrowed, as our language has been, from a great variety of sources, to which it is desirable ever to retain the means of tracing it, there is certainly much apparent lack of correspondence between its oral and its written form. Still the discrepancies are few, when compared with the instances of exact conformity; and, if they are, as I suppose they are, unavoidable, it is as useless to complain of the trouble they occasion, as it is to think of forcing a reconciliation. The wranglers in this controversy, can never agree among themselves, whether orthography shall conform to pronunciation, or pronunciation to orthography. Nor does any one of them well know how our language would either sound or look, were he himself appointed sole arbiter of all variances between our spelling and our speech.

OBS. 3.—"Language," says Dr. Rush, "was long ago analyzed into its alphabetic elements. Wherever this analysis is known, the art of teaching language has, with the best success, been conducted upon the rudimental method." * * * "The art of reading consists in having all the vocal elements under complete command, that they may be properly applied, for the vivid and elegant delineation of the sense and sentiment of discourse."—*Philosophy of the Voice*, p. 346. Again, of "the pronunciation of the alphabetic elements," he says, "The least deviation *from the assumed standard* converts the listener into the critic; and I am surely speaking within bounds when I say, that for every miscalled element in discourse, ten succeeding words are lost to the greater part of an audience."—*Ibid.*, p. 350. These quotations plainly imply both the practicability and the importance of teaching the pronunciation of our language analytically by means of its present orthography, and agreeably to the standard assumed by the grammarians. The first of them affirms that it has been done, "with the best success," according to some ancient method of dividing the letters and explaining their sounds. And yet, both before and afterwards, we find this same author complaining of our alphabet and its subdivisions, as if sense or philosophy must utterly repudiate both; and of our orthography, as if a ploughman might teach us to spell better: and, at the same time, he speaks of softening his censure through modesty. "The deficiencies, redundancies, and confusion, of the system of alphabetic characters in this language, prevent the adoption of its subdivisions in this essay."—*Ib.*, p. 52. Of the specific sounds given to the letters, he says, "The first of these matters is under the rule of every body, and therefore is very properly to be excluded from the discussions of that philosophy which desires to be effectual in its instruction. How can we hope to establish a system of elemental pronunciation in a language, when great masters in criticism condemn at once every attempt, in so simple and useful a labour as the correction of its orthography!"—P. 256. Again: "I *deprecate noticing* the faults of speakers, in the pronunciation of the alphabetic elements. It is better for criticism to be modest on this point, till it has the sense or independence to make our alphabet and its uses, look more like the work of what is called—wise and transcendent humanity: till the pardonable variety of pronunciation, and the *true spelling by the vulgar*, have satirized into reformation that pen-craft which keeps up the troubles of orthography for no other purpose, as one can divine, than to boast of a very questionable merit as a criterion of education."—*Ib.*, p. 383.

OBS. 4.—How far these views are compatible, the reader will judge. And it is hoped he will excuse the length of the extracts, from a consideration of the fact, that a great master of the "pen-craft" here ridiculed, a noted stickler for needless Kays and Ues, now commonly rejected, while he boasts that his grammar, which he mostly copied from Murray's, is teaching the old explanation of the alphabetic elements to "more than one hundred thousand children and youth," is also vending under his own name an abstract of the new scheme of "*tonicks, subtonicks,* and *atonicks*;" and, in one breath, bestowing superlative praise on both, in order, as it would seem, to monopolize all inconsistency. "Among those who have successfully laboured in the philological field, *Mr. Lindley Murray* stands forth in bold relief, as undeniably at the head of the list."—*Kirkham's Elocution*, p. 12. "The modern candidate for oratorical fame, stands on very different, and far more advantageous, ground, than that occupied by the young and aspiring Athenian; especially since a *correct analysis of the vocal organs,* and a faithful record of their operations, have been given to the world by *Dr. James Rush,* of Philadelphia—a name that will *outlive* the unquarried marble of our mountains."—*Ibid.,* p. 29. "But what is to be said when presumption pushes itself into the front ranks of elocution, and thoughtless friends undertake to support it? The fraud must go on, till presumption quarrels, as often happens, with its own friends, or with itself, and thus dissolves the spell of its merits."—*Rush, on the Voice,* p. 405.

OBS. 5.—The question respecting the *number* of simple or elementary sounds in our language, presents a remarkable puzzle: and it is idle, if not ridiculous, for any man to declaim about the imperfection of our alphabet and orthography, who does not show himself able to solve it. All these sounds may easily be written in a plain sentence of three or four lines upon almost any subject; and every one who can read, is familiar with them all, and with all the letters. Now it is either easy *to count* them, or it is difficult. If difficult, wherein does the difficulty lie? and how shall he who knows not what and how many they are, think himself capable of reforming our system of their alphabetic signs? If easy, why do so few pretend to know their number? and of those who do pretend to this knowledge, why are there so few that agree? A certain verse in the seventh chapter of Ezra, has been said to contain all the letters. It however contains no *j*; and, with respect to the sounds, it lacks that of *f,* that of *th sharp,* and that of *u* in *bull.* I will suggest a few additional words for these; and then both all the letters, and all the sounds, of the English language, will be found in the example; and most of them, many times over: "'And I, even I, Artaxerxes, the king, do make a decree to all the treasurers' who 'are beyond the river, that whatsoever Ezra the priest, the scribe of the law of the God of heaven, shall require of you, it be done speedily' and faithfully, according to that which he shall enjoin." Some letters, and some sounds, are here used much more frequently than others; but, on an average, we have, in this short passage, each sound five times, and each letter eight. How often, then, does a man speak all the elements of his language, who reads well but one hour!

OBS. 6.—Of the number of elementary sounds in our language, different orthoëpists report differently; because they cannot always agree among themselves, wherein the identity or the simplicity, the sameness or the singleness, even of well-known sounds, consists; or because, if each is allowed to determine these points for himself, no one of them adheres strictly to his own decision. They may also, each for himself, have some peculiar way of utterance, which will confound some sounds which other men distinguish, or distinguish some which other men confound. For, as a man may write a very bad hand which shall still be legible, so he may utter many sounds improperly and still be understood. One may, in this way, make out a scheme of the alphabetic elements, which shall be true of his own pronunciation, and yet have obvious faults when tried by the best usage of English speech. It is desirable not to multiply these sounds beyond the number which a correct and elegant pronunciation of the language obviously requires. And what that number is, it seems to me not very difficult to ascertain; at least, I think we may fix it with sufficient accuracy for all practical purposes. But let it be remembered, that all who have hitherto attempted the enumeration, have deviated more or less from their own decisions concerning either the simplicity or the identity of sounds; but, most commonly, it appears to have been thought expedient to admit some exceptions concerning both. Thus the long or diphthongal sounds of *I* and *U*, are admitted by some, and excluded by others; the sound of *j*, or soft *g*, is reckoned as simple by some, and rejected as compound by others; so a part, if not all, of what are called the long and the short vowels, as heard in *ale* and *ell*, *arm* and *am*, *all* and *on*, *isle* or *eel* and *ill*, *tone* and *tun*, *pule* or *pool* and *pull*, have been declared essentially the same by some, and essentially different by others. Were we to recognize as elementary, no sounds but such as are unquestionably simple in themselves, and indisputably different in quality from all others, we should not have more sounds than letters: and this is a proof that we have characters enough, though the sounds are perhaps badly distributed among them.

OBS. 7.—I have enumerated *thirty-six* well known sounds, which, in compliance with general custom, and for convenience in teaching. I choose to regard as the oral elements of our language. There may be found some reputable authority for adding four or five more, and other authority as reputable, for striking from the list seven or eight of those already mentioned. For the sake of the general principle, which we always regard in writing, a principle of universal grammar, *that there can be no syllable without a vowel*, I am inclined to teach, with Brightland, Dr. Johnson, L. Murray, and others, that, in English, as in French, there is given to the vowel *e* a certain very obscure sound which approaches, but amounts not to an absolute suppression, though it is commonly so regarded by the writers of dictionaries. It may be exemplified in the words *oven, shovel, able*;[99] or in the unemphatic article *the* before a consonant, as in the sentence, "Take the nearest:" we do not hear it as "*thee nearest*," nor as "*then carest*," but more obscurely. There is also a feeble sound of *i* or *y* unaccented, which is equivalent to *ee* uttered feebly, as in the word *diversity*. This is the most common sound of *i* and of *y*. The vulgar are apt to let it fall into the more obscure sound of short *u*. As elegance of utterance depends much upon the preservation of this sound from such obtuseness, perhaps Walker and others have done well to mark it as *e* in *me*; though some suppose it to be peculiar, and others identify it with the short *i* in *fit*. Thirdly, a distinction is made by some writers, between the vowel sounds heard in *hate* and *bear*, which Sheridan and Walker consider to be the same. The apparent difference may perhaps result from the following consonant *r*, which is apt to affect the sound of the vowel which precedes it. Such words as *bear, care, dare, careful, parent*, are very liable to be corrupted in pronunciation, by too broad a sound of the *a*; and, as the multiplication of needless distinctions should be avoided, I do not approve of adding an other sound to a vowel which has already quite too many. Worcester, however, in his new Dictionary, and Wells, in his new Grammar, give to the vowel A *six* or *seven* sounds in lieu of *four*; and Dr. Mandeville, in his Course of Reading, says, "A has *eight* sounds."—P. 9.

OBS. 8.—Sheridan made the elements of his oratory *twenty-eight*. Jones followed him implicitly, and adopted the same number.[100] Walker recognized several more, but I know not whether he has anywhere told us *how many there are*. Lindley Murray enumerates *thirty-six*, and the same thirty-six that are given in the main text above. The eight sounds not counted by Sheridan are these: 1. The Italian *a*, as in *far, father*, which he reckoned but a lengthening of the *a* in *hat*; 2. The short *o*, as in *hot*, which he supposed to be but a shortening of the *a* in *hall*; 3. The diphthongal *i*, as in *isle*, which he thought but a quicker union of the sounds of the diphthong *oi*, but which, in my opinion, is rather a very quick union of the sounds *ah* and *ee* into *ay, I*;[101] 4. The long *u*, which is acknowledged to be equal to *yu* or *yew*, though perhaps a little different from *you* or *yoo*,[102] the sound given it by Walker; 5. The *u* heard in *pull*, which he considered but a shortening of *oo*; 6. The consonant *w*, which he conceived to be always a vowel, and equivalent to *oo*; 7. The consonant *y*, which he made equal to a short *ee*; 8. The consonant *h*, which he declared to be no letter, but a mere breathing, In all other respects, his scheme of the alphabetic elements agrees with that which is adopted in this work, and which is now most commonly taught.

OBS. 9.—The effect of *Quantity* in the prolation of the vowels, is a matter with which every reader ought to be experimentally acquainted. *Quantity* is simply the *time* of utterance, whether long or short. It is commonly spoken of with reference to *syllables*, because it belongs severally to all the distinct or numerable impulses of the voice, and to these only; but, as vowels or diphthongs may be uttered alone, the notion of quantity is of course as applicable to them, as to any of the more complex sounds in which consonants are joined with them. All sounds imply time; because they are the transient effects of certain percussions which temporarily agitate the air, an element that tends to silence. When mighty winds have swept over sea and land, and the voice of the *Ocean* is raised, he speaks to the towering cliffs in the deep tones of a *long* quantity; the rolling billows, as they meet the shore, pronounce the long-drawn syllables of his majestic elocution. But see him again in gentler mood; stand upon the beach and listen to the rippling of his more frequent waves: he will teach you *short* quantity, as well as long. In common parlance, to avoid tediousness, to save time, and to adapt language to circumstances, we usually utter words with great rapidity, and in comparatively short quantity. But in oratory, and sometimes in ordinary reading, those sounds which are best fitted to fill and gratify the ear, should be sensibly protracted, especially in emphatic words; and even the shortest syllable, must be so lengthened as to be uttered with perfect clearness: otherwise the performance will be judged defective.

OBS. 10.—Some of the vowels are usually uttered in longer time than others; but whether the former are naturally long, and the latter naturally short, may be doubted: the common opinion is, that they are. But one author at least denies it; and says, "We must explode the pretended natural epithets *short* and *long* given to our vowels, independent on accent: and we must observe that our silent *e* final lengthens not its syllable, unless the preceding vowel be accented."—*Mackintosh's Essay on E. Gram.*, p. 232. The distinction of long and short vowels which has generally obtained, and the correspondences which some writers have laboured to establish between them, have always been to me sources of much embarrassment. It would appear, that in one or two instances, sounds that differ only in length, or time, are commonly recognized as different elements; and that grammarians and orthoëpists, perceiving this, have attempted to carry out the analogy, and to find among what they call the long vowels a parent sound for each of the short ones. In doing this, they have either neglected to consult the ear, or have not chosen to abide by its verdict. I suppose the vowels heard in *pull* and *pool* would be necessarily identified, if the former were protracted or the latter shortened; and perhaps there would be a like coalescence of those heard in *of* and *all*, were they tried in the same way, though I am not sure of it. In protracting the *e* in *met,* and the *i* in *ship,* ignorance or carelessness might perhaps, with the help of our orthoëpists, convert the former word into *mate* and the latter into *sheep*; and, as this would breed confusion in the language, the avoiding of the similarity may perhaps be a sufficient reason for confining these two sounds of *e* and *i*, to that short quantity in which they cannot be mistaken. But to suppose, as some do, that the protraction of *u* in *tun* would identify it with the *o* in *tone*, surpasses any notion I have of what stupidity may misconceive. With one or two exceptions, therefore, it appears to me that each of the pure vowel sounds is of such a nature, that it may be readily recognized by its own peculiar quality or tone, though it be made as long or as short as it is possible for any sound of the human voice to be. It is manifest that each of the vowel sounds heard in *ate, at, arm, all, eel, old, ooze, us,* may be protracted to the entire extent of a full breath slowly expended, and still be precisely the same one simple sound;[103] and, on the contrary, that all but one may be shortened to the very minimum of vocality, and still be severally known without danger of mistake. The prolation of a pure vowel places the organs of utterance in that particular position which the sound of the letter requires, and then *holds them unmoved* till we have given to it all the length we choose.

OBS. 11.—In treating of the quantity and quality of the vowels, Walker says, "The first distinction of sound that seems to obtrude itself upon us when we utter the vowels, is a long and a short sound, according to the greater or less duration of time taken up in pronouncing them. This distinction is so obvious as to have been adopted in all languages, and is that to which we annex *clearer ideas than to any other*; and though the short sounds of some vowels have not in our language been classed with sufficient accuracy with their parent long ones, yet this has bred but little confusion, as vowels long and short are always sufficiently distinguishable."—*Principles*, No. 63. Again: "But though the terms long and short, as applied to vowels, are pretty generally understood, an accurate ear will easily perceive that these terms do not always mean the long and short sounds of the respective vowels to which they are applied; for, if we choose to be directed by the ear, in denominating vowels long or short, we must certainly give these appellations to those sounds only which have *exactly the same radical tone,* and differ only in the long or short emission of that tone."—*Ib.*, No. 66. He then proceeds to state his opinion that the vowel sounds heard in the following words are thus correspondent: *tame, them; car, carry; wall, want; dawn, gone; theme, him; tone,* nearly *tun; pool, pull.* As to the long sounds of *i* or *y,* and of *u,* these two being diphthongal, he supposes the short sound of each to be no other than the short sound of its latter element *ee* or *oo.* Now to me most of this is exceedingly unsatisfactory; and I have shown why.

OBS. 12.—If men's notions of the length and shortness of vowels are the clearest ideas they have in relation to the elements of speech, how comes it to pass that of all the disputable points in grammar, this is the most perplexed with contrarieties of opinion? In coming before the world as an author, no man intends to place himself clearly in the wrong; yet, on the simple powers of the letters, we have volumes of irreconcilable doctrines. A great connoisseur in things of this sort, who professes to have been long "in the habit of listening to sounds of every description, and that with more than ordinary attention," declares in a recent and expensive work, that "in every language we find the vowels *incorrectly classed*"; and, in order to give to "the simple elements of English utterance" a better explanation than others have furnished, he devotes to a new analysis of our alphabet the ample space of twenty octavo pages, besides having several chapters on subjects connected with it. And what do his twenty pages amount to? I will give the substance of them in ten lines, and the reader may judge. He does not tell us *how many* elementary sounds there are; but, professing to arrange the vowels, long and short, "in the order in which they are naturally found," as well as to show of the consonants that the mutes and liquids form correspondents in regular pairs, he presents a scheme which I abbreviate as follows. VOWELS: 1. *A*, as in *=all* and *wh~at*, or *o*, as in *orifice* and *n~ot*; 2. *U—=urn* and *h~ut*, or *l=ove* and *c~ome*; 3. *O—v=ote* and *ech~o*; 4. *A— =ah* and *h~at*; 5. *A—h=azy*, no short sound; 6. *E—=e=el* and *it*; 7. *E— m=ercy* and *m~et*; 8. *O—pr=ove* and *ad~o*; 9. *OO—t=o=ol* and *f~o~ot*; 10. *W—vo=w* and *la~w*; 11. *Y—*(like the first *e—*) *s=yntax* and *dut~y*. DIPHTHONGS: 1. *I—*as *ah-ee*; 2. *U—*as *ee-oo*; 3. *OU—*as *au-oo*. CONSONANTS: 1. Mutes,—*c* or *s*, *f*, *h*, *k* or *q*, *p*, *t*, *th sharp*, *sh*; 2. Liquids, —*l*, which has no corresponding mute, and *z*, *v*, *r*, *ng*, *m*, *n*, *th flat* and *j*, which severally correspond to the eight mutes in their order; 3. Subliquids, —*g hard*, *b*, and *d*. See "Music of Nature," by *William Gardiner*, p. 480, and after.

OBS. 13.—Dr. Rush comes to the explanation of the powers of the letters as the confident first revealer of nature's management and wisdom; and hopes to have laid the foundation of a system of instruction in reading and oratory, which, if adopted and perfected, "will beget a similarity of opinion and practice," and "be found to possess an excellence which must grow into sure and irreversible favour."—*Phil. of the Voice*, p. 404. "We have been willing," he says, "*to believe, on faith alone*, that nature is wise in the contrivance of speech. Let us now show, by our works of analysis, how she manages the *simple elements* of the voice, in the production of their unbounded combinations."—*Ibid.*, p. 44. Again: "Every one, with peculiar self-satisfaction, thinks he reads well, and yet all read differently: there is, however, *but one mode* of reading well."—*Ib.*, p. 403. That one mode, some say, his philosophy alone teaches. Of that, others may judge. I shall only notice here what seems to be his fundamental position, that, on all the vocal elements of language, nature has stamped duplicity. To establish this extraordinary doctrine, he first attempts to prove, that "the letter *a*, as heard in the word *day*," combines two distinguishable yet inseparable sounds; that it is a compound of what he calls, with reference to vowels and syllables in general, "the radical and the vanishing movement of the voice,"—a single and indivisible element in which "two sounds are heard continuously successive," the sounds of *a* and *e* as in *ale* and *eve*. He does not know that some grammarians have contended that *ay* in *day* is a proper diphthong, in which both the vowels are heard; but, so pronouncing it himself, infers from the experiment, that there is no simpler sound of the vowel a. If this inference is not wrong, the word *shape* is to be pronounced *sha-epe*; and, in like manner, a multitude of other words will acquire a new element not commonly heard in them.

OBS. 14.—But the doctrine stops not here. The philosopher examines, in some similar way, the other simple vowel sounds, and finds a beginning and an end, a base and an apex, a radical and a vanishing movement, to them all; and imagines a sufficient warrant from nature to divide them all "into two parts," and to convert most of them into diphthongs, as well as to include all diphthongs with them, as being altogether as simple and elementary. Thus he begins with confounding all distinction between diphthongs and simple vowels; except that which he makes for himself when he admits "the radical and the vanish," the first half of a sound and the last, to have no difference in quality. This admission is made with respect to the vowels heard in *ooze, eel, err, end,* and *in,* which he calls, not diphthongs, but "monothongs." But in the *a* of *ale,* he hears =*a'-ee*; in that of *an,* ~*a'-~e*; (that is, the short *a* followed by something of the sound of *e* in *err*;) in that of *art, ah'~-e*; in that of *all, awe'-~e*; in the *i* of *isle,* =*i'-ee*; in the *o* of *old,* =*o'-oo*; in the proper diphthong *ou, ou'-oo*; in the *oy* of *boy,* he knows not what. After his explanation of these mysteries, he says, "The seven radical sounds with their vanishes, which have been described, include, as far as I can perceive, all the elementary diphthongs of the English language."—*Ib.,* p. 60. But all the sounds of the vowel *u,* whether diphthongal or simple, are excluded from his list, unless he means to represent one of them by the *e* in *err*; and the complex vowel sound heard in *voice* and *boy,* is confessedly omitted on account of a doubt whether it consists of two sounds or of three! The elements which he enumerates are thirty-five; but if *oi* is not a triphthong, they are to be thirty-six. Twelve are called "*Tonics*; and are heard in the usual sound of the separated *Italics,* in the following words: A-ll, *a*-rt, *a*-n, *a*-le, *ou*-r, *i*-sle, *o*-ld, *ee*-l, *oo*-ze, *e*-rr, *e*-nd, *i*-n,"—*Ib.,* p. 53. Fourteen are called "*Subtonics*; and are marked by the separated Italics, in the following words: *B*-ow, *d*-are, *g*-ive, *v*-ile, *z*-one, *y*-e, *w*-o, *th*-en, a-*z*-ure, si-*ng*, *l*-ove, *m*-ay, *n*-ot, *r*-oe."—*Ib.,* p. 54. Nine are called "*Atonics*; they are heard in the words, U-*p*, ou-*t*, ar-*k*, i-*f*, ye-*s*, *h*-e, *wh*-eat, *th*-in, pu-*sh*."—*Ib.,* p. 56. My opinion of this scheme of the alphabet the reader will have anticipated.

Milton Keynes UK
Ingram Content Group UK Ltd.
UKHW032018090124
435730UK00013B/372